T0334645

Cambridge Elements ≡

Elements on Women in the History of Philosophy
edited by
Jacqueline Broad
Monash University

VICTORIA WELBY

Emily Thomas
Durham University

CAMBRIDGE
UNIVERSITY PRESS

Shaftesbury Road, Cambridge CB2 8EA, United Kingdom

One Liberty Plaza, 20th Floor, New York, NY 10006, USA

477 Williamstown Road, Port Melbourne, VIC 3207, Australia

314–321, 3rd Floor, Plot 3, Splendor Forum, Jasola District Centre, New Delhi – 110025, India

103 Penang Road, #05–06/07, Visioncrest Commercial, Singapore 238467

Cambridge University Press is part of Cambridge University Press & Assessment, a department of the University of Cambridge.

We share the University's mission to contribute to society through the pursuit of education, learning and research at the highest international levels of excellence.

www.cambridge.org
Information on this title: www.cambridge.org/9781009345866

DOI: 10.1017/9781009345897

First published 2023

A catalogue record for this publication is available from the British Library.

ISBN 978-1-009-34586-6 Paperback
ISSN 2634-4645 (online)
ISSN 2634-4637 (print)

Victoria Welby

Elements on Women in the History of Philosophy

DOI: 10.1017/9781009345897
First published online: February 2023

Emily Thomas
Durham University
Author for correspondence: Emily Thomas, emily.e.thomas@durham.ac.uk

Abstract: In 1880s Britain, Victoria Welby (1837–1912) began creating a rich, wide-ranging metaphysical system. At its heart lies Motion, 'the great fact, the supreme category'. Drawing extensively on archive materials, this Element offers the first study of Welby's metaphysics. It portrays her universe as a complex of motions: motions comprise material bodies, living beings, and conscious minds. This dynamic universe, 'Motion', underlies many other elements of her thought, including her views on idealism, panpsychism, change, space, and anti-realism about time. This study shows that Welby's metaphysics are deeply embedded in the scientific–philosophical debates of her period, and variously draw on vortex theories of matter in physics; Victorian panpsychisms, fuelled by debates over the continuity of mind in Darwinian evolution; and new conceptions of time as the 'fourth dimension' of space. *Victoria Welby* significantly advances our understanding of Welby's philosophy, opening paths for future scholarship.

This Element also has a video abstract: www.cambridge.org/victoriawelby

Keywords: Victoria Welby, historical women philosophers, Victorian metaphysics, panpsychism, time

ISBNs: 9781009345866 (PB), 9781009345897 (OC)
ISSNs: 2634-4645 (online), 2634-4637 (print)

Contents

1 Introducing Welby's Metaphysics

Victoria Welby (1837–1912) began working on metaphysics in 1880s Britain, a heady period which saw scientists and philosophers grappling with new theories of matter, evolution, and space. This Element offers the first study of her metaphysical system. At its core lies a grand ontology of Motion, befitting Welby's remarks on the subject. 'Motion', she writes, 'is that "reality" to which all else is subordinate'.[1] 'I am and always was an essentially dynamic thinker', 'Motion is my governing idea'.[2] 'The thesis of motion as primary runs through all my thinking.'[3] 'Motion is the great fact, the supreme category.'[4] On my reading of Welby, what we usually think of as the material universe is merely a complex of motions: motions comprise material bodies, living beings, and conscious minds. Welby labels this dynamic universe 'Motion' (I follow her practice of capitalising Motion in this sense). Motion underlies her views on matter, mind, idealism, space, change, and time; Motion even points us towards God.

This study will show that Welby's metaphysical theories are grounded in the science of her day. 'My thought', she explains in an 1887 letter, 'fits in with the best attested facts of modern science'.[5] To explain her theories, it is often necessary to explain how they are powered by poorly studied debates in physics and biology. As such, this Element advances our understanding of Welby, *and* of the neglected Victorian science she engaged with, including vortex theories of matter, Darwin-driven panpsychisms, and 'fourth dimensional' accounts of time. When Welby's metaphysics are pieced together, we will see that they form a rich, intricate, wide-ranging system – one that carefully navigates the tangled jungles of Victorian philosophy *and* science.

This Element proceeds as follows. Section 2 gives some background on Welby and her philosophical works. The subsequent sections enquire into Welby's metaphysics, tracing the development of her views in rough chronological order. Using texts from the mid-1880s onwards, Section 3 starts with Welby's 'supreme' metaphysic of Motion, explaining how she conceives material bodies as motions. I argue her account of Motion draws on the work of various scientists: vortex matter theorists George Romanes, G. Johnstone Stoney, Karl Pearson, and William Armstrong. Section 4 explores Welby's account of minds as motions, an account which hints at how minds might be

---

[1] Untitled note dated 28 April 1907; see VWF, 1970–010/032–01.
[2] Manuscript dated 7 April 1907, headed 'Prof. Stout'; see VWF, 1970–010/032–12. It likely formed part of a letter to G. F. Stout.
[3] Letter to Frederick Pollock dated 18 July 1907; see VWF, 1970–010/013.
[4] Untitled note dated 29 April 1907; see VWF, 1970–010/032–01.
[5] Letter to Norman Pearson dated December 1887; see VWF, 1970–010/012.

immortal. Section 5 argues that Welby's metaphysic of Motion is ultimately idealist. Focusing on 1890–1 texts, Section 6 argues Welby held a panpsychism akin to that of W. K. Clifford and C. Lloyd Morgan. Yet, on my reading, Welby's position is complicated by her willingness to acknowledge genuine novelty within nature. I argue her resulting struggle runs parallel to that found in the mature emergentism of Lloyd Morgan and Samuel Alexander, and the layered picture of reality she arrives at is especially similar to that of Alexander. Section 7 considers Welby's views on time across her career, arguing that from her earliest, 1881 writings on the topic she posits a block universe; and that from around 1897 she arrives at a complementary, new position, that time is derivative on space. Welby publishes this metaphysic in her 1907 *Mind* article 'Time as Derivative'. Section 8 investigates Welby's identification, from around 1897, of Motion with space. I argue that Welby's Motion-Space can profitably be understood using Clifford's identification of matter with the curvature of space. Section 9 concludes by summarising my understanding of Welby's metaphysical system, and speculating on the relationship between Motion and God. Welby's metaphysics, and the shadowy scientific–philosophical debates underlying them, reward exploration.

2 Sketching Welby's Life and Works

Lady Victoria Alexandrina Maria Louisa Welby, née Stuart-Wortely, was born into the British aristocracy: her godmothers were Princess Victoria (later, Queen Victoria) and the Duchess of Kent (the Queen mother). Following early years of travel abroad, and two years spent at the court of Queen Victoria, Welby married Sir William Welby-Gregory and retired to Denton Manor, Grantham (Lincolnshire). After the death of her husband in 1898, Welby moved to Duneaves, Harrow (London).[6] Her wide-ranging interests included philosophy, language, theology, science, technology, education, and literature. Evidence of this breadth can be found in the newspaper clippings she collected, and often annotated. To give just a few examples, these clippings include articles on 'Motor-Car Engineering'; 'Medicine To-Day'; 'Automatic [Telephone] Exchange'; 'Woman Suffrage and Its Advocates'; 'Quackery and Dental Clinics'; and 'The Sources of Energy', on radium and coal.[7]

From the 1860s until her death, Welby maintained an extensive intellectual network, corresponding with over 450 figures. These figures include major philosophers and scientists of the period, such as Henri Bergson, F. H. Bradley,

---

[6] These and other biographical details are taken from Eschbach (1983, ix–xv), Schmitz (1985, xxii–xxviii), Myers (1995, 1–5), and Petrilli (2009, 7–14).

[7] VWF, 1970–010/38.

Shadworth Hodgson, T. H. Huxley, William James, Christine Ladd-Franklin, Vernon Lee, Charles Sanders Peirce, Bertrand Russell, F. C. S. Schiller, G. F. Stout, and Mrs Humphry Ward. From 1886 she became close friends with Lucy Clifford, novelist and widow of philosopher W. K. Clifford (who died in 1879). In her memoriam of Welby, Lucy Clifford (1924, 106) wrote, 'She knew everyone who counted in the world.' Welby used her network to develop ideas and to bring people together, putting her correspondents in contact with each other, and hosting events.[8] She even offered the 'Welby Prize' for the best essay on 'significs', her label for theories of meaning, which was published by the journal *Mind* in 1896. In a 1901 parody edition of the journal, *Mind!*, her friend Schiller immortalised the event with characteristic slapstick style:

> LADY WELBY, whose interest in clearing up intellectual fogs and purifying the philosophical atmosphere is well known, has offered a prize of £1,000 to any philosopher who can produce adequate documentary evidence to show that he:
> (1) Knows what he means.
> (2) Knows what any one else means. (Schiller, 1901, 128)

Schiller's comic announcement indicates that, by 1901, Welby was already 'well known' amongst her peers.

A fraction of Welby's correspondence has been published; I recount the major efforts here.[9] Welby's daughter, Mrs Henry Cust, published two volumes of letters spanning 1879–1911; see Cust (1929, 1931). These volumes are extremely valuable but they have drawbacks: Cust silently edited some of the prose, and does not include precise dates for each letter.[10] Decades later, Charles S. Hardwick (1977) published Welby's 1903–11 correspondence with Peirce. Susan Petrilli's (2009) groundbreaking study of Welby, *Signifying and Understanding*, includes additional unpublished correspondence, alongside some of Welby's unpublished essays and more inaccessible publications. Despite these efforts, the vast bulk of Welby's correspondence – and many draft papers – remains unpublished in the Lady Victoria Welby Fonds at York University, Ontario (VWF).

Welby published many articles, and several books, during her lifetime. Most of her publications concern language, and she is best known for her 1903 *What Is Meaning?*. Peirce (repr. in Hardwick, 1977, 157) praised this book as 'really

---

[8] On her networking, see especially Hardwick (1977, xxix), Eschbach (1983, xiv), and Schmitz (2013).

[9] Schmitz (2013) details many more minor efforts to publish Welby's letters, for example in the collected correspondence of other figures.

[10] For a fuller description of these volumes, and their problems, see Schmitz (2013, 205–6).

important', comparing it with Bertrand Russell's *Principles of Mathematics*.[11] Eschbach (1983, xvi) claims this shows that Peirce held Welby in high esteem – 'far higher esteem than many Peirce scholars, who make only occasional mention of Lady Welby and then frequently in footnotes as the correspondence partner of the great semiotics expert'. Happily, following a fallow period in the mid-twentieth century, interest in Welby picked up from the 1970s. This was partly due to the Hardwick (1977) volume; and partly to Eschbach's (1983) edition of *What Is Meaning?*, which included a lengthy editorial introduction. Two years later, Schmitz (1985) edited a collection on her work, *Essays on Significs: papers presented on the occasion of the 150th anniversary of the birth of Victoria Lady Welby, 1837–1912*. Today, partly spurred by Petrilli's ongoing scholarship, interest in Welby's work on language continues. Not least, Nuessel et al. (2013) edited a special issue of the journal *Semiotica* on Welby's significs.

Likely because *What Is Meaning?* and the Peirce–Welby correspondence focus on language, Welby is frequently characterised as primarily (even exclusively) focused on language. For example, Schmitz (1985, xii) records that 1920s scholars describe Welby as an early investigator of meaning. Hardwick (1977, xix) writes, 'From 1885 until her death in 1912, Lady Welby's interests were almost completely centred on problems of language and meaning.' Peijnenburg and Verhaegh (forthcoming) describe Welby as a philosopher 'of language'. Yet historians of philosophy are slowly becoming interested in other aspects of Welby's work. For example, Misak (2016, 82–5), Metzer (2020), and Hurley (2022) study Welby's relationship with pragmatism; Pearson (forthcoming) explores Welby's views on analytic philosophy and education; and Stone (forthcoming) examines Welby's views on meaning *and* naturalism. Against prevailing characterisations of Welby as being uninterested in metaphysics, I have argued that Welby offers a metaphysical idealism, and an anti-realist metaphysic of time; see Thomas (forthcoming a, forthcoming b).

With the exception of her articles on time, I find that whilst Welby's publications hint at deep metaphysical views, they offer no detail. Yet, through archival research, I have found that *hundreds* of her unpublished letters and manuscripts concern metaphysics. I draw extensively on these materials to construct my reading of Welby's system. There is evidence that Welby wanted to publish her views. One of Welby's (repr. in Petrilli, 2009, 36–7) plans for future books include chapters on 'motion and the dynamic, instead of Matter and the static'; the 'self'; and 'Time as distinctly derived from Space as Room + motion, Change and succession'. Sadly, these plans did not come to pass, and her

---

[11] Peirce reviewed both books in the same three-page article but dispensed with *The Principles of Mathematics* in a single paragraph.

metaphysics largely remains in the archives. This Element aims to reconstruct the system she might have advanced. Venturing deep into the wilds of Welby's thought, it seeks to dispel any lingering doubts as to her interest in metaphysics. Future scholars may dispute my reading of Welby's metaphysical system but not, I hope, that she *has* one.

3 Material Bodies as Motions

3.1 Introducing Welby's Puzzling Claims on Matter and Motion

Lucy Clifford (1924, 101–2) sheds light on the chronology of Welby's intellectual development when she recalls a trip they took to Switzerland in 1886: 'it was soon evident that she was in a transition stage, dreaming and evolving theories of her own, reaching out towards the thinkers – humbly seeking knowledge from them and encouragement to pursue her own tracks of thought'. I find it highly plausible that 1886 was a 'transition stage' for Welby, for her metaphysical claims emerge forcibly from that year onwards.

From around that period, Welby repeatedly states that 'Motion', or the 'dynamic', is prior to matter. Here are some examples. The following passage is taken from an 1886–8 letter to theologian W. H. Simcox:

> We know now what we never knew before, that, beyond all we see as 'fixed' or 'stationary', there is Motion – in every molecule as in every solar-system.
> (Welby, repr. in Cust, 1929, 202)

This is from an 1889–90 letter to another theologian, Edmund McClure:

> I have had certain ideas all or nearly all my life which I am now finding day by day to be in unexpected general correspondence with the present lines of scientific advance ...
> [Including] Replacement of the static by the dynamic. Everywhere for a lump of stuff called 'substance', read a complex of energy. The 'stuff' is always secondary and provisional; the motion is always primary and permanent. (Welby, repr. in Cust, 1929, 265–6)

In *What Is Meaning?*, Welby (1983 [1903], 174) reiterates that 'Motion' and the 'dynamic' are primary, whilst 'Matter' and the 'static' are secondary.

Welby's 1907 'Time as Derivative' claims that, once we have improved our conception of Motion:

> the term 'matter' will be reduced to its proper function of indicating content and resistance. Whatever resists, whatever is contained, is the outcome of that ultimate dynamic order which in the last resort is the source of the static or at least its governing pre-supposition. (Welby, 1907, 398)

I have found a 1902 draft of 'Time as Derivative', which adds:

> we postulate matter at rest and then conceive Motion as coming to shove it
> on ... But we have to reverse this if we take the view here suggested. It is
> Motion which 'constructs' Matter.[12]

Finally, consider this passage from a letter to William James, dated 24 May 1908:

> Having lost or failed to gain the sense of the supremacy of motion over its
> product matter, and of the solidity attained by intensely rapid, minute, con-
> fined motion (of some 'third' element, apparently 'ether'?), we make a ruling
> fetish of stuff, although in English we couple it with *nonsense*.
>
> (Welby, repr. in Petrilli, 2009, 59)

In the absence of further explanation, these statements are puzzling, even
obscure. I argue we can best understand them by looking to Welby's engagement with the physics of her period.

3.2 Welby's Engagement with Vortex Theories of Matter

A major milestone of Victorian physics was the development of 'field theories'.
On these theories, phenomena such as electromagnetism are derived from
a more fundamental medium – a field. From the 1860s, William Thomson
(later, Lord Kelvin) developed a new kind of field theory: the 'vortex' theory
of matter. Earlier thinkers had suggested that electromagnetic waves, including
light, travelled through an undetectable, space-filling field or substance known
as 'ether'. Building on this, Thomson (1867, 15–17) argued we should stop
conceiving material atoms as 'strong and infinitely rigid pieces of matter'.
Instead, we should conceive them as 'vortex atoms', akin to moving vortices
within liquid. Thomson compares vortex atoms with the rings of smoke produced by cigars or cigarettes. He records recently witnessing a 'magnificent
display of smoke-rings', wherein the rings bounced off each other, 'shaking
violently from the effects of the shock', yet elastically maintaining their shape.
Vortex atoms are, however, more complex than smoke-rings: although
Thomson conceives them roughly as rings, a closed loop with two ends meeting,
these atoms can be 'knotted or knitted' in many different ways. He argues that
the variety of vortices, and their interplay, could potentially explain all material
phenomena.[13]

---

[12] VWF, 1970–010/032–03.

[13] The notion that material bodies are not really rigid pieces of matter has a long philosophical
history. For example, Kant's 1786 *Metaphysical Foundations of Natural Science* describes
material bodies in terms of attractive and repulsive forces; see Watkins and Stan (2014, §2.3).
Yet, as far as I am aware, these vortex theorists did not draw on this history.

Thomson's vortex theory of matter had a huge impact on late-nineteenth-century British science. In her pioneering study of its history, Doran (1975, 197) explains that this 'program for a field theory of matter ... was widely subscribed to in Britain by 1880'. Physicist Oliver Lodge (1883b, 329–30) described Thomson's theory as 'highly beautiful', 'the simplest conception of the material universe which has yet occurred', a theory which almost 'deserves to be true'. Lodge (who would later defend his own vortex theory) usefully summarises how it was understood in the early 1880s:

> We must begin to imagine a continuous connecting medium between the particles – a substance in which they are imbedded, and which extends ... without break to the remotest limits of space ...
>
> Gravitation is explainable by differences of pressure in the medium ...
>
> Light consists of undulation or waves in the medium; while electricity is turning out quite possibly to be an aspect of a part of the very medium itself.
>
> The medium is now accepted as a necessity by all modern physicists ...
>
> The name you choose to give to the medium is a matter of very small importance, but 'the Ether' is as good a name for it as another.
>
> (Lodge, 1883a, 305)

Of especial interest to us is how physicists understood Thomson's theory of matter:

> whirling portions [of ether] constitute what we call matter; their motion gives them rigidity, and of them our bodies and all other material bodies with which we are acquainted are built up.
>
> One continuous substance filling all space ... which in whirls constitutes matter ... This is the modern view of the ether and its functions.
>
> (Lodge, 1883b, 330)

Just as motions in water create whirlpools, motions in another medium create material bodies. As Lodge's description exemplifies, some vortex theorists explicitly conceive matter as *motions of ether*. However, others simply conceive matter as *motions*; implying either that there is no underlying medium, or else leaving the nature of the underlying medium open. Some of these latter, motion-focused accounts drew on Thomson's (1884, 204) statement: 'it is scarcely possible to help anticipating ... the arrival at a complete theory of matter, in which all its properties will be seen to be merely attributes of motion'. This section will now set out three texts defending vortex theories of matter.[14]

The first is G. Johnstone Stoney's 1885 paper, 'How Thought Presents Itself in Nature'. Stoney was an Irish physicist, best known for his work on light,

---

[14] There is very little literature on the vortex atomism of these particular texts, but Doran's study (1975, 249, 198) briefly mentions that the work of Stoney and Pearson forms part of this tradition.

gases, the solar system, and for advancing towards the discovery of the 'electron' – a term he coined.[15] In the introduction to this paper, Stoney (1885, 178–9) explains that science has shown the universe to exhibit greater 'simplicity' than previously realised. The simplicities he identifies all concern motion. For example, 'Sound is Motion', such as vibrating piano strings; and 'Light is Motion', for we see objects via motions in the molecules affecting our retinas. Stoney (1885, 186–7) states that force, mass, and energy are merely 'functions of the motions'. Our bodies comprise motions, including the vibrations of nerve fibres, and 'intricate' movements within the brain. He claims there need not be any 'mysterious entity' called 'substance': we need not accept that 'underlying every motion must be some *thing* to be moved'. He summarises these findings as follows:

> we are confronted with the fact revealed to us by science, that every phenomenon of the outer world which we can perceive by any of our senses, is simply a mass of motions . . .
>   scientific inquiry finds motion pervading the material universe; motion everywhere, motions underlying every phenomenon, and it finds *nothing existing outside the mind excepting motions*. (Stoney, 1885, 189, 191)

For Stoney, science shows that the material universe is really 'a mass of motions'.

The second is George Romanes' 1885 paper, 'Mind and Motion'. Romanes was a Canadian-Scots evolutionary biologist, best known for his work on the nervous system, natural selection, and mental evolution.[16] The paper declares:

> [It is] a matter of carefully demonstrated fact, that all our knowledge of the external world is nothing more than a knowledge of motion. For all the forms of energy have now been proved to be but modes of motion; and even matter, if not in its ultimate constitution vortical motion, at all events is known to us only as changes of motion. . . . We do not even know what it is that moves; we only know that when some modes of motion pass into other modes, we perceive what we understand by matter. (Romanes, 1885, 75–6)

For Romanes, matter is only known to us as 'changes of motion'.

The third text is Karl Pearson's 1892 *The Grammar of Science*. Pearson was an English mathematician and philosopher, best known for 'almost single-handedly' establishing the discipline of mathematical statistics.[17] As its title indicates, *The Grammar of Science* is partly concerned with scientific language: Pearson (1892, viii) aims to address the 'obscurity' enveloping scientific principles. However, it also makes many claims about matter. Some of these claims

---

[15] See Owen and O'Hara (2004).   [16] See Smith (2004).   [17] See Woiak (2004).

were foreshadowed in another book Welby owned: Pearson's 1888 *The Ethic of Freethought*.[18] For example, this text states:

> The scientific view of the physical universe . . . is based simply on motion . . .
> The popular conception of matter, as a hard, dead something, is merely
> a superstition. The very essence of matter is motion. (Pearson, 1888, 66–7)

But *The Grammar of Science* discusses matter in far more detail. In a chapter titled 'Matter', Pearson (1892, 330) claims that, for many thinkers, the 'notion of matter' is 'obscure'. Against the 'commonsense' conception of matter as 'impenetrable' atoms, Pearson (1892, 304–5) argues that other conceptions are available. He considers 'a wave on the surface of the sea', as in Figure 1. Waves

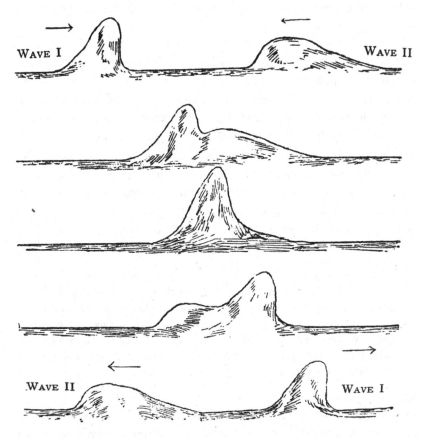

Figure 1 Waves moving across the sea. Taken from Pearson (1900, 256). This image is in the public domain; it is reproduced (with permission) from a copy at Durham University Library

---

[18] See The Lady Welby Library catalogue, University of London.

maintain their identity as they travel across water, suggesting another conception of matter:

> [One] reason for citing this wave example lies in the light it throws on the possibilities involved in the statement: '*Matter is that which moves*'. The wave consists of a particular form of motion in the substratum [i.e. the water] which for the time constitutes the wave. This form of motion itself moves along the surface of the water. Hence we see that beside the substratum something else can be conceived as moving, namely, *forms of motion*. What if, after all, matter as the moving thing could be best expressed in conception by a form of motion moving. (Pearson, 1892, 307)

On this theory, the water does not move; what moves is the wave, a 'form of motion'. For Pearson, a material body is like a wave: it is not an impenetrable particle, but a form of motion.

Over commonsense conceptions of matter, Pearson (1892, 309–10) prefers ether theories: 'it is the great hope of science at the present day that "hard and heavy matter" will be shown to be ether in motion'. If we could account for all our 'sense-impressions of hardness, weight, colour, temperature, cohesion', and so on via 'the motions of a single medium', our scientific descriptions would be 'immensely simplified'. Pearson (1892, 317–18) goes on to explain that, on Thomson's account of vortex atoms as rings, 'the substratum of an atom always consists of the same elements of moving ether'. Just as a smoke-ring always consists of the same smoke molecules, Thomson seems to conceive vortex atoms as always consisting of the same parts of the ether. Against this, Pearson offers an alternative account. Ocean waves need not consist of the same seawater molecules, and the same goes for vortex atoms:

> [I] put forward a theory in which, while the ether is still looked upon as a perfect fluid, the individual atom does not always consist of the same elements of ether. In this theory an atom is conceived to be a point at which ether flows in all directions into space; such a point is termed an *ether-squirt*. An ether-squirt in the ether is thus something like a tap turned on under water . . . the ether-squirt seems a conceptual mechanism capable of describing a very considerable range of phenomenon.
>
> (Pearson, 1892, 318–19)

For Pearson, vortex atoms are *squirts* – modes of motion. If we turned on a tap underwater, Pearson (1892, 320–1) explains that 'the pressure produced by the flow of water' might produce 'new sense-impressions' in the region of the squirt – the water might seem 'hard and impenetrable'. 'Such squirts, although only water in motion, might form very *material* groups of sense-impressions.' Pearson speculates that the squirts originate in a fourth dimension of space; to explain this, he cites the novel *Flatland*.

We perceive three spatial dimensions – length, width, and depth – but mathematicians have long theorised more. Charles Hinton's 1880s work popularised theories of the 'fourth dimension', likely inspiring Edwin Abbott's 1884 novel *Flatland* (initially published under the memorable pseudonym, 'A. Square'). *Flatland* describes creatures that can only perceive limited numbers of spatial dimensions: Linelanders perceive one; Flatlanders perceive two; whilst we humans, Spacelanders, perceive three. Abbott (1884, x) writes that, just as Flatlanders struggle conceive the third dimension, Spacelanders struggle to conceive the 'Fourth unrecognised Dimension ... called by no name at present'. Pearson (1892, 322–3) rightly notes that for some years 'four-dimensioned space' has 'formed the subject of elaborate investigations by some of our best mathematicians'. His speculation, that if we could travel 'out through' ether squirts we would arrive in a higher dimension, is 'intended for those minds which ... cannot wholly repress their metaphysical tendencies'.

With this scientific background in place, let's return to Welby. I have set out these particular defences of vortex atoms because Welby engaged closely with all three of them. (As she corresponded at length with Lodge, from 1895 to 1911, she was likely familiar with his pertinent works too, but I have not yet found evidence of this.[19]) Welby's copy of Stoney's 'How Thought Presents Itself in Nature' is well annotated, and she underlines its claim that all phenomena is 'simply a mass of motions'.[20] She also took notes on Stoney's 1903 'On the Dependence of What Apparently Takes Place in Nature upon What Actually Occurs in the Universe of Real Existences', which advocates for many of the same theses; interestingly, these notes seem to address Stoney directly. As Welby corresponded with Stoney in 1905,[21] these notes may actually be a letter. They show that she accepted his account of matter:

> I have of course all my life seen that the only accessible reality for us consists entirely of Motions and their analogues. ... The idea of 'material substance' I have always seen to be a sometimes convenient but else indefensible postulate. Recognised as strictly secondary it may have its uses but unfortunately we treat it as a fact on the same level of reality as motion. Now objects, as you say, consist of 'almost inconceivably minute and swift motions'; they are 'masses of internal motion'; and this 'motion' is the 'key' to the nature of experience.[22]

When Welby states that motion constructs body, I believe this is precisely what she has in mind.

Welby also took notes on Romanes' 'Mind and Motion', stressing 'Motion the ultimate fact' (emphasis in original).[23] This article prompted her to write to

---

[19] VWF, 1970–010/009.   [20] VWF, 1970–010/22–09.   [21] VWF, 1970–010/15.

[22] VWF, 1970–010/022–02.   [23] VWF, 1970–010/22–03.

Romanes, and they corresponded intermittently from 1887 to 1892. In her first letter, dated 11 March 1887, Welby writes that she has 'been very much struck' by 'Mind and Motion', and it corresponds with 'long cherished ideas of my own'.[24] They met for the first time shortly afterwards. In a letter to Vernon Lee dated 31 March 1887, Welby writes, 'since my last visit to London and the long talks there with ... Mr Romanes, and others among the younger and "coming" thinkers ... my work has entered on a fresh stage'.[25]

Welby also hugely admired Pearson's *Grammar of Science*, which she read by at least March 1892.[26] In a letter to the 'Vicar of Leeds', likely authored in 1892,[27] she writes of it:

> This book of Karl Pearson's I feel in a certain sense cuts my work into two periods ... the one before, the one after it. It is a tremendous leaf to have turned ... [I have produced] one hundred closely written pages of 'notes' upon it. (Welby, repr. in Cust, 1929, 279)

I have found forty-four of those pages, comprising extracts from *The Grammar of Science*, and Welby's notes on its 'main positions'.[28] Welby clearly distinguishes her views from Pearson's using brackets and blue chalk. As you would expect, she praises Pearson for reconsidering 'the right use of language', adding that the book 'may be considered as virtually an Essay in practical "Semantics"'. Yet she also comments on his theory of matter. Of Pearson's thesis that the notion of matter is 'obscure', Welby writes, 'These are words of which it is difficult to exaggerate the importance.' Of his conception of matter as forms of motion, Welby writes, 'And here as elsewhere I find scientifically expressed and described what for years has been at the spring of all my thinking.' She notes that Thomson and Pearson's conceptions of atoms are *both* valuable, for both stress 'activity', not 'substance', with regard to 'matter'. Of Pearson's view that science would be simplified if we could account for 'matter' via 'motion', Welby writes that this would be 'significant'. Of Pearson's speculation regarding the fourth dimensional origin of ether, Welby writes, 'Instead of recoiling from, we have to penetrate the materialist's cobweb "barrier," – which falls at the sound of the author's trumpet, – and come out at the further "side".' Welby evidently felt that Pearson's view offered a means of rejecting materialism; I'll say on more on this in Section 5.

---

[24] VWF, 1970–010/013–18.

[25] Frustratingly from a scholarly perspective, Welby adds, 'though I shrink from publication no less than I did before'; see VWF, 1970–010/011–30.

[26] In a letter to Shadworth Hodgson dated 11 March 1892, Welby writes that she is 'enjoying' the book; see VWF, 1970–010/007–02.

[27] Cust dates the letter to 1889–91 but Pearson's *Grammar* was not published until 1892 (and there can be no doubt that Welby's letter is referring to Pearson's *Grammar*, as she quotes from it).

[28] VWF, 1970–010/22–06.

Welby tried several times to strike up a correspondence with Pearson, asking him for mathematical advice in 1887; and sporadically raising topics such as *The Grammar of Science* and *What Is Meaning?* from 1903 to 1911. However, he politely declined to engage with her.[29]

Given Welby's deep involvement with these three texts, I argue they are at least partly responsible for what Lucy Clifford called Welby's 'transition stage', during which she evolved 'theories of her own'. It is to those theories that we now turn.

3.3 Welby's Metaphysic of Motion

Stoney, Romanes, Pearson, and many other Victorian scientists argued in various ways that matter is motion. I read Welby as defending this thesis. Against this background, many of her above remarks about Motion cease to be puzzling. Traditionally, material bodies such as tables and rocks are conceived as stable lumps of matter – as 'static'. Yet vortex theories of matter conceived material bodies as motions – as 'dynamic'. If the vortex theorists are correct, then it is reasonable to claim that the dynamic is prior to the static, that motion 'constructs' matter. Of course there is motion in every molecule of the solar system: material molecules *are* motion. And, punning on the English expression 'stuff and nonsense', it is no surprise to find Welby arguing that our 'ruling fetish of stuff' is 'nonsense': ultimately, stuff does not exist, there is only motion.

This reading helps us understand many further texts in Welby. For example, in a letter to British empiricist Shadworth Hodgson dated 12 October 1891, Welby writes of motion:

> My favourite illustration here is of the homeliest. The more rigidly you wish to sustain a [spinning] top in fixity of place and position, the more you must intensify its motion. Slacken that, and at once it inclines this way and that, and – wobbles! This therefore is the type of steadiness I want ... ever before 'entity' comes 'mode of motion'.[30]

A spinning top is more stable the faster it spins. Analogously, Welby is arguing that the more intense the motion, the more rigid the resulting entity.

At some point before March 1892, Welby loaned her friend the lawyer and philosopher Norman Pearson a 'Proceedings' by Stoney – given the date, this was likely 'How Thought Presents Itself in Nature'. In a letter dated 9 March 1892, Pearson returned the paper, and raises a worry for it: 'Mr Stoney does not dispose of the difficulty which he partly admits i.e. motions

---

[29] VWF, 1979–010/012. [30] VWF, 1970–010/007–02.

imply something that move, and what is this something.' Returning to this issue in a letter dated 10 October 1892, Welby implicitly affirms a commitment to 'the idea of motion as apart from a thing which moves'. She adds, 'Stoney, K. Pearson, O. Lodge &c put what I mean much better than I can: in this case I know I am "on the crest of a rising tide"!'. As Welby found Karl Pearson's thesis that matter comprises modes of motion, on which no 'thing' moves, to be a scientific expression of 'what for years has been at the spring of all my thinking', she almost certainly has this thesis in mind. As *The Grammar of Science* illustrates this thesis using ocean waves, Welby's 'rising tide' metaphor may be a private joke.

A few weeks later, in a letter dated 1 November 1892, Welby writes to Norman Pearson:

> Science tells us more and more emphatically that if we carry investigation into matter (or 'substance') far enough, we find ourselves compelled to express it in terms of motion. Now, however far we may carry the analysis or scrutiny of motion, we never find ourselves describing <u>that</u> in terms of matter or substance – or stuff! If we did, we should speedily arrive not only at <u>stuff</u> but at the <u>nonsense</u> associated with it in popular lingo! . . . I fall back upon Johnston Stoney as my best spokesman.

In a letter dated 8 January 1893, Welby draws Norman Pearson's attention to an article in *Mind*, which she paraphrases as follows: 'all we perceive is movement and . . . it is an inherited fallacy that there must be something moved!'.[31] On this, she comments approvingly, 'Hear hear'.

Assuming this reading of Welby on Motion is correct, it raises a question. What *is* Motion? Possibly, Welby conceives it as ether: her 1908 letter to James refers to rapid motions 'of some "third" element, apparently "ether"?'. Yet the question mark indicates that this suggestion is tentative. I argue we should read Welby's conception of Motion as energy. To make this case, I'll start with the textual evidence that hints towards this reading. For example, as we saw in Section 3, Welby's 1889–90 letter to McClure states that we should replace 'substance' with 'a complex of energy'. Similarly, in a letter to novelist and lobbyist Mrs Humphry Ward dated 15 May 1887, Welby writes:

> [I]n the very nature of things there can be no 'fundamental basis' and no permanent fixity . . .
> that 'void' in which there is not even an atmosphere in which to breathe . . .
> is in the last resort just all the foundation which we (in our world-total) have.

---

[31] I believe Welby is referring to an anonymous (1893, 129) book review, which describes 'the obstinate tendency of mankind to believe that there cannot be movement without something moved', yet 'All we perceive is movement'.

> That which safely bears us in the gulfs of space [i.e. the Earth] is no base or
> basis, no moveless central 'rock', but throbbing energies in complex and
> manifold action, in swing and wave and thrill: whirling us onward in mighty
> sweeps of rhythm.[32]

This passage conceives our planet, a material body, as a collection of *energies*. If
matter is motion, and matter is also energy, then Welby may conceive motion as
energy.

Earlier in this Element we saw that 'Time as Derivative' makes a related claim –
that matter indicates resistance. Explaining this requires some background. Several
Victorian philosophers held that we only experience matter as resistance. For
example, Herbert Spencer (1862, 232–3) claims our primary experience of matter
is 'resistance', such as door opposing our 'muscular energies'. He understands
resistance as 'Force'. Spencer (1862, 251) identifies Force with the subject of the
scientific principle the 'Conservation of Force', better known today as the
'Conservation of Energy'; Victorians sometimes used the terms 'force' or 'energy'
interchangeably.[33] In an article published during September 1886 that likely draws
on Spencer, Norman Pearson (1886, 360) agrees that 'our primary notion of matter
is simply of something which offers resistance to muscular energy'. Furthermore,
he understands resistance as Force: 'That which opposes force must be itself force.'
Welby was familiar with the work of both men, and she wrote to Pearson about this
article specifically.[34] Given this, I read the claim that 'matter' indicates 'resistance'
as meaning that 'matter' indicates force or energy.

Hints aside, I find compelling evidence that Welby conceives Motion as
energy in her engagement with the work of another vortex matter theorist. In
1897, Lord William Armstrong published *Electric Movement in Air and Water:
With Theoretical Inferences*.[35] As Armstrong (1897b, 6) explains, the larger part
of this book uses photography to illustrate 'electric effects hitherto invisible and
unknown', such as photographing electric discharges through water. It is the
smaller, 'theoretical' part of the book that interests us. Armstrong (1897a, 8–9)
accepts 'Lord Kelvin's [Thomson's] views on vortex atoms', on which 'vortex
motion must be the most universal of all motions'. He continues:

> It may well be doubted whether molecules themselves are anything more than
> specialised motions. ... Lord Kelvin ... has said, 'It is scarcely possible to

---

[32] VWF, 1970–010/019–05. A version of this letter is published in Cust (1929, 173).

[33] To illustrate, both terms can be found in Stewart and Taite's (1875, 80) vintage history of the
principle of the conservation of energy.

[34] In a letter to Norman Pearson dated 20 October 1886, Welby wrote that the article is of 'great
interest to me'; see VWF, 1970–010/012. A version of this letter is published in Cust (1929, 18).

[35] Heald's (2011, 237–40) biography of Armstrong provides a rare discussion of this book – or, as
she describes it, of Armstrong's 'last great masterpiece'.

> help anticipating the arrival of a complete theory of matter in which all its properties will be seen to be nearly attributes of motion.' But motion of what? At present we assume the existence of ether to supply the supposed need of a subject, and also able to fill up gaps in continuity. But is it easier to conceive a continuity of ether than a continuity of interacting motions? I confess my inability to judge, but we are more familiar with motion than with ether, and we do not seem to gain much by postulating two inscrutables instead of one ... Motion would then stand forth as the 'absolute' of matter. (Armstrong, 1897a, 53–4)

Armstrong suggests that material molecules are motions. Yet, he asks, must we assume they are motions *of ether*? This passage describes 'motion' *and* 'ether' as 'inscrutable', unknowable. As they are both inscrutable, Armstrong asks whether we 'gain much' by positing two inscrutables, rather than one. We are 'more familiar' with motion: we experience it, and it is well-studied by science. In contrast, ether cannot be experienced, or even observed by science. Consequently, he suggests we posit motion *only*.

Armstrong (1897b, 6) expanded on these remarks in *The Times*, explaining that his characterisation of molecules as motions is *not* equivalent to saying 'that we can have motion without anything being moved'. He accepts that motion assumes 'something to pass from place to place'. But what is that something? Armstrong's answer is energy: 'It may be questionable whether we can properly call energy a "thing"; but there can be no doubt that it is a reality which moves and does work.' He argues this answer is preferable to material 'corpuscles', which are 'unsupported by any reliable evidence'; and to ether, because 'motion in conjunction with energy is a fact, while ether is only a hypothesis'.

In Armstrong's thinking, Welby found confirmation of her own. On 15 February 1898, she wrote to him saying so.[36] As this unpublished letter is so important, I quote from it at length:

> Lord Armstrong,
>   I feel sure you will excuse the liberty I take in addressing you although a stranger, when I explain that the view which you set forth in your wonderful book on 'Electric Movement' and in a letter to the Times, has been to me all my life the only natural one.
>   I am entirely without mathematical or scientific training. But the fact that a woman from her earliest years has instinctively taken the view now scientifically expressed in the 'structural capacity of motion', in the definition of the molecules of matter as modes of motion, and of motion as the 'absolute' of matter, may itself have some slight psychological interest for you. Lord Kelvin had of course struck what was for me the same familiar note:

---

[36] For all their extant correspondence, see VWF, 1970–010/001.

only I felt as you do that 'we do not seem to gain much by postulating two inscrutables instead of one'.

My main interest in the matter however is a practical one. If this view of nature can be through early education brought home to the general mind: if we begin to realise that the concept of Motion is really primary and that of Matter secondary: that the popular view of Matter needs reversing ... then a tremendous revolution in thought must begin also, extending far beyond the limits of physics or mechanics, indeed throughout human experience itself...

But I must resist the temptation to enlarge further on what to me is a fascinating theme: and hoping I have not unduly troubled you remain,

Lady Welby

This letter confirms my reading of Welby's account of material bodies or molecules as 'modes of motion'. For Welby, modes of Motion move, without requiring things that move. It also introduces a new thesis: Welby is sceptical of positing two 'inscrutables' – two unknown entities – instead of one. Like Armstrong, she would prefer to posit 'interacting motions' only, and not posit 'ether'. This counts against reading Motion as ether, and in favour of reading Motion as energy.

On 21 February 1898, Armstrong's nephew wrote to Welby, explaining that his uncle was too ill to reply personally. However, Armstrong wished to convey his thanks for her 'extremely able' letter, and that it gave him 'a great pleasure to find that a lady could grasp so fully and with so much intelligence the nature of so recondite a subject'. Later, in a letter dated 21 March 1899, of which only a fragment survives, Armstrong sympathises with Welby's 'sad loss' (presumably of her husband, who died on 26 November 1898) and adds, 'from the tenor of your former admirable letter to me, I felt that there was a kindred intellectual link between us'. Welby clearly agreed.

To summarise, Welby's metaphysic of Motion is drawn from Victorian vortex theories of matter, on which material bodies are motions. Welby's universe is a swirling complex of motions – of energy. This is why, in a charming postcard to Schiller dated 15 November 1903, she describes leaves as follows: 'the leaf and its fellows as ultimately aught but varieties of Energy'.[37]

4 Minds as (Immortal) Motions

On my reading of Welby, it is not just material bodies that are motions. Minds, our very selves, are *also* motions. There is ample textual evidence in support of this interpretation, and I find that Welby's remarks on the mind and self remain consistent from the mid-1880s onwards. Here are some examples.

---

[37] VWF, 1970–010/014–07.

In an 1886–8 letter to Henry Drummond, Welby writes:

> Dynamical for statical is the key. We have thought of the 'I' (of personal identity) as a thing, a substance, an entity. We must learn to think of it as an energy, an act, a movement. (Welby, repr. in Cust, 1929, 196)

And in a 1889–90 letter to Edmund McClure:

> I have always felt, e.g., that I was no lump, but a movement. . . . Now that I know I am a furnace and not, so to express it, a box of fuel, I am content. (Welby, repr. in Cust, 1929, 265–6)

In her notes on James Sully's 1892 *The Human Mind: A Text-Book of Psychology*, Welby critiques Sully for failing to take the new science of matter into account:

> Mind has always been expressed in terms of matter. But now 'matter' is dethroned by science: we must redefine it in terms of Motion.[38]

And her 1902 draft of 'Time as Derivative' states:

> [I]t may even be said that we <u>are</u> essentially 'motion' in its highest, the vital, volitional, moral forms; our ideas of life, of will, of motive, of 'mental energy', of 'spiritual activity' are all primarily those of what in physics we call velocity.[39]

Finally, Welby's unpublished essay, 'A Significant Question' dated 26 August 1903, states: 'matter and mind' are both 'products' of 'Motion'.[40] As I read Welby, all these passages are claiming that, just as material bodies are really motions, so too are minds. 'I' am a movement, not a substance.

I find confirmation of this reading in a number of further passages where Welby illustrates her understanding of mind, self, or spirit using the process of breathing. Her 1891 article 'Breath and the Name of the Soul' notes that the English term 'spirit' is etymologically rooted in the Latin *spirare*, to breathe. It asks why this is so, and suggests:

> [A] possible explanation of the choice of breath (or pulse) as the main term for animal or vital energy, which, in accordance with the whole drift of modern thought, is given in terms of the dynamic instead of the static. The 'spirit' is thus no entity but a rhythm, a beat, a thrill, a sequence of throbs . . . the earliest and simplest thought was . . . of giving motion and not matter the primary place in trying to express the essential 'self' or 'soul' of things.
>
> (Welby, 1891, 2894–5)

The process of breathing comprises 'a rhythm, a beat'. Welby is suggesting that, by connecting the self with breathing, early thinkers conceived spirit as motion

---

[38] VWF, 1970–010/022–8.　　[39] VWF, 1970–010/032–03.　　[40] VWF, 1970–010/031–10.

rather than matter. She makes a similar point in another article, published the following year:

> [H]ere also we have to ... advance ... to a dynamic, instead of a static, view of the world, and again enthrone motion as at once the primary and the ultimate fact ...
>
> Take 'spirit', meaning breath. This needs a book to itself never yet written. But meanwhile even now it may be remarked that we use the words 'a spirit' ... as in some sense a motive force or spring of energy. ... And, after all, breath is first (like pulse) a *rhythm*. (Welby, repr. in Petrilli, 2009, 231)

For Welby, *we* are motions, complexes of energy, so it follows that we would use the process of breathing – a rhythmic motion – to describe the spirit.

Fascinatingly, Welby claims that her understanding of the mind allows for a new understanding of immortality. Many Victorians sought an account of the immortality of the mind that would be compatible with science. For example, as Asprem (2011, 142) explains, physicists Balfour Stewart and Peter Guthrie Taite used the ether to defend the existence of vast realms beyond this world, sustaining Christian notions of deity, the spiritual body, and an afterlife. Romanes' 'Mind and Motion' (1885, 92) also hints at human immortality, writing that although we only know the human mind as associated with brain, that does not mean 'that mind cannot exist in any other mode'.

Welby's claim regarding immortality occurs in a letter to Hodgson, dated 17 June 1900:

> [I]f you make Breath the spirit (as the governing idea of the world of consciousness) you are taking the 'motion first' position. ...
>
> Thus if instead of the nervous system viewed so to speak as a skeleton of nerves ready to be dissected, we start from the complex of nervous energies. ... And this will have an enormous influence, though one little as yet realised, upon our thoughts of immortality.
>
> A ripple cannot be 'destroyed' in the same sense that a group of particles can, a symphony does not break up in the same sense that an organism does.[41]

Much of what Welby writes here is familiar: we should conceive the mind or spirit as 'breath', as a movement; and, when we take this 'motion first' position, we will rightly perceive our nervous system as a complex of energies. What is unfamiliar is the notion that this will affect our understanding of immortality. Welby does not explain precisely what she means but I offer a reading grounded in her engagement with the work of Karl Pearson.

---

[41] VWF, 1970–010/007–03.

I find Welby's claim that 'a group of particles' can be destroyed, whilst a 'ripple' cannot, reminiscent of the section in *The Grammar of Science* where Pearson offers his new wave account of matter. It is titled 'Individuality does not denote Sameness in Substratum', and it critiques the 'commonsense' conception of matter as impenetrable atoms. Pearson (1892, 304–6) claims, 'It does not follow of logical necessity that because we experience the same group of sense-impressions at different times and in different places, or even continuously, that there must be one and the same thing at the basis of these sense-impressions.' He stresses that a wave 'may retain its form' across the sea, preserving its 'individual characteristics', even though the water composing it changes: 'its substratum may be continually changing'. This process is depicted in Figure 1. In her notes on this passage in *The Grammar of Science*, Welby writes that although the wave is no 'unchangeable individual something', it seems 'as perceptually real as if it were': 'we can watch its "advance," identifying it from moment to moment, as though it were an "object" like the bits of sea-weed it leaves behind'.[42]

We know that Welby conceives material bodies as waves, as modes of motion, and there is some evidence she conceives the mind or self in the same way. For example, in the Contents of *What Is Meaning?*, Welby (1983 [1903], xvii) summarises her position as follows: 'Motion [is] our paramount analogy', 'For "we are all waves"'. If minds are akin to waves, then a new account of immortality suggests itself. As Welby accepts, a wave can travel across the sea, and we can identify it from moment to moment, yet its substratum is continually changing. Similarly, if the mind or self is a wave, it would not depend for its existence on our mortal bodies – its substratum could change. In this sense, ripples cannot be destroyed.

5 Idealism: Motion as Spirit

Idealism is a family of positions holding that reality comprises something mental, such as mind, spirit, or experience.[43] Alison Stone and I have both previously argued that Welby should be read as an idealist, grounding our readings on Welby's correspondence with novelist Eliza Lynn Linton.[44] This section approaches Welby's idealism from an entirely new tack, arguing that her position is akin to the idealisms defended by several vortex matter theorists. By conceiving material bodies as motions, these Victorian physicists are already

---

[42] VWF, 1970–010/22–06.

[43] On idealism and its history more generally, see Guyer and Horstmann (2021, §1).

[44] Focusing on the Welby-Linton correspondence, Thomas (forthcoming a) compares Welby's position with that of Spencer and T. H. Huxley, and argues her idealism is rooted in religion. Using the same correspondence, Stone (forthcoming) argues that Welby's idealism has an affinity with that of Annie Besant's theosophy.

some distance from traditional materialism. And, as Asprem (2011, 138) explains, this allows them to question what matter really *is*. For some, the answer is 'thought'.[45] To make my case, I'll set out the views of the vortex matter theorists we know Welby engaged with.

Let's start with Stoney. 'How Thought Presents Itself in Nature' comprises two inquiries, and thus far we have only discussed the 'scientific' one. Here we will discuss the second. Stoney (1885, 192–3) writes that this 'falls not within the domain of science but of metaphysics'. Stoney claims that whilst 'we know not' what motions 'are in themselves', there is 'considerable evidence' that they are 'thought':

> not our thought, but thought that is going on elsewhere than in our consciousness. For this hypothesis, the simplest that can be entertained, quite gets rid of what is else an oppressive difficulty, the abrupt appearance of thought. On the hypothesis now put forward the thought which is associated with a brain would be no 'Jack in the box', springing up suddenly before us, but would be in full consonance with *the ordinary course of nature ...*
>
> the thoughts of which we are conscious as our mind, and are aware of as minds in our fellow-men and in other animals are in reality very small swirls in an illimitable ocean of thought. (Stoney, 1885, 193)

On her copy of this paper, Welby underlines and stars all these lines.[46] Stoney is arguing for a kind of idealism on which the material universe comprises motion, and motion comprises thought. Human and animal minds comprise 'small swirls' of motion in this larger universe. He argues this hypothesis solves an 'oppressive difficultly': the 'appearance' of thought. It will prove helpful to explain this difficulty in some detail.

Charles Darwin's 1859 *Origin of Species* prompted scientists to ask whether the process of evolution is continuous throughout nature. In his important study of philosophical engagement with evolution, Blitz (1992, 9–12) explains that many evolutionists believed that nature could not, by itself, make the jumps required to produce 'novelties' such as minds or consciousness. This led to two widely held positions. Naturalists held that minds are produced by nature. As nature cannot make jumps, this pushed Darwin and others towards 'panpsychism', the position that mind or mentality is not a novelty, but is somehow present throughout nature. In contrast, supernaturalists held that minds are novelties, and they are not present throughout nature; minds appear in nature through divine intervention. Defending the latter view, Alfred Russell Wallace (1895, 209) presented it as the only

---

[45] On the idealisms of vortex matter theorists, see also Hunt (1992, 97–100). Asprem and Hunt both discuss the idealisms of Stoney and Lodge. On Romanes' account of the mind, see Blitz (1992, 50–6) and Forsdyke (2015).

[46] VWF, 1970–010/22–09.

acceptable horn of a dilemma: 'There is no escape from this dilemma, – either all matter is conscious, or consciousness is . . . something distinct from matter.' I follow Blitz (1992, 46) in labelling this 'Wallace's dilemma': evolutionists must choose panpsychism or supernaturalism. Stoney evidently embraces the panpsychist horn of Wallace's dilemma: mind does not spring up from nowhere, rather it is consonant with nature because it is everywhere.

Romanes' 'Mind and Motion' – which Welby described as corresponding with her own 'long cherished ideas' – advances related theses. In the context of arguing against mind-motion (i.e. mind-matter) dualism, Romanes (1885, 88–9) argues we should identify mind with motion: 'any change taking place in the mind, and any corresponding changes taking place in the brain, are really not two changes, but one change'. Also plumping for panpsychism, Romanes reasons that wherever there is motion (i.e. wherever there is matter) there could be mind. It is unsurprising to find Romanes reasoning along these lines, for he also upheld Darwin's belief in the continuity of nature; towards the end of his life, Darwin became close friends with Romanes. An 1886 article in *The Times* went so far as to describe Romanes as 'the biological investigator upon whom in England the mantle of Mr. Darwin has most conspicuously descended'.[47]

Finally, whilst Armstrong does not explicitly defend idealism, he inclines towards it. 'These views of the structural capacity of motion', Armstrong (1897a, 54) writes, 'present Nature under a more spiritual aspect than one of crude Materialism . . . they make her appear more akin to an Infinite Dominant Mind'. Like Romanes and Stoney, it seems that Armstrong's metaphysic of motion leads him to conceive nature not as material, but as mental or spiritual.

Several of Welby's texts imply she also conceives the universe in an idealist way. One is a letter she wrote to Linton, dated 7 November 1886:

> You have not got hold as yet of my ideas as to materialism. <u>I do not believe that there is any such thing.</u> . . . All we know of 'matter' as Norman Pearson points out is <u>resistance.</u> Now as Spirit is ultimate Energy it implies resistance: that is, the idea of 'matter' lies within that of 'spirit'.[48]

As we saw in Section 3.3, Spencer and Norman Pearson claim that all we know of 'matter' is force or energy. Neither man understands force or energy to be material.[49] As I read this passage, Welby is arguing that all we know of matter is energy; as spirit is the 'ultimate Energy', spirit includes matter.

---

[47] See Smith (2004).

[48] VWF, 1970–010/009–16. A version of this letter is published in Cust (1929, 175).

[49] Spencer (1862, 483) rejects labelling reality 'matter' *or* 'mind', for neither 'can be taken as ultimate'. In a letter to Welby dated 9 March 1892, Norman Pearson writes that he shares Stoney's view that what we know as matter 'is mind . . . up to a certain point'; see VWF, 1970–010/012.

This is why she does not believe there is 'any such thing' as materialism. Fundamentally, the universe is spirit, not matter. This is a kind of idealism. Putting this together with my understanding of Welby's Motion as energy, if spirit is the 'ultimate Energy', then I suggest that Welby's Motion is spirit. This reading of Welby's Motion would be in the same vein as the idealisms of Stoney and Romanes.

Another pertinent text is a letter Welby wrote to humanist Leslie Stephen, dated 21 February 1893. Commenting on Stephen's 1893 defence of atheism, *An Agnostic's Apology*, she writes:

> You rightly speak of 'so flimsy a thing as a soul' (p. 153). But its flimsiness obviously depends on the analogy of <u>matter</u>; and it is inapplicable in the presumably truer one of <u>motion</u> ...
>
> What if it [the soul] be rather that of a complex of 'motions' or 'movements', of a group of activities, of a sum of co-ordinated impulses or waves or thrills? ... [Suppose] that 'matter' at best was but the equivalent of the 'theatre' of spiritual activity: that on which or through it works or plays?[50]

We know that Welby's Motion produces matter. If spirit works 'through' matter, then, again, it seems likely that Welby identifies Motion with spirit.

This brings us to our final text, a letter Welby wrote to Schiller, dated 12 November 1903:

> The true meaning of spirit is the spirit e.g. of justice, of injustice, of enterprise, of routine, &c.; in short it is simply an impellent, an impulse of energy: the motor, for good or evil, of human life. The Holy Spirit thus becomes the moving and governing force – the Prime Mover.[51]

This passage describes spirit as 'an impulse of energy', as something that impels. Again, this suggests the identification of Motion with spirit. Although it does not give further details, it hints that the Christian Holy Spirit should be understood as the 'Prime Mover' – Aristotle's first cause. We will briefly return to this religious angle in Section 9. Here, I just stress again that, for Welby, Motion is energy *and* spirit.

6 Panpsychism: 'Mind-Activity' and Novelty in Nature

6.1 Clifford, Lloyd Morgan, and Welby's 'Mind-Activity'

On Welby's system, what is the place of mind in nature? I argue she is best read as a panpsychist (a reading which, as we shall see, confirms her idealism).

---

[50] VWF, 1970–010/015–16. A version of this letter is published in Cust (1931, 21–3), where it is erroneously dated 1898–1902.

[51] VWF, 1970–010/014–07. A version of this letter is published in Cust (1931, 107).

The first two parts of this section show that, in 1890–1, Welby advocates a panpsychism akin to that of W. K. Clifford and Lloyd Morgan. Yet, complicating her position, Welby *also* conceives mind as a novelty exclusively belonging to a higher level of nature. The final part of this section considers Welby's intellectual network with regard to these issues.

Let's start by explaining the Victorian backdrop that Welby was working against. In Section 5, we saw that Stoney and Romanes were pushed towards panpsychism by their belief in the continuity of evolution. This belief is rooted in Darwin's (1859, 194) *Origin of Species*, which claimed 'natural selection can act only by taking advantage of slight successive variations; she can never take a leap'. Applying the maxim that nature cannot make jumps to humans, Darwin's (1871, 105) *Descent of Man* claimed that 'the difference in mind between man and the higher animals, great as it is, is certainly one of degree and not of kind'. Even faculties such as 'self-consciousness', which seem 'peculiar' to humans, may be 'incidental results of other highly advanced intellectual faculties'. Here, we will see that Darwinian faith in evolutionary continuity also motivates the panpsychisms of Clifford and Lloyd Morgan.

Clifford's position emerges in his paper 'On the Nature of Things-in-Themselves', delivered in 1874 and published in *Mind* four years later. Affirming the continuity of evolution, Clifford (1878, 64) argues that evolution displays 'a series of imperceptible steps connecting inorganic matter with ourselves'. It is 'impossible' to point out 'any sudden break' in these steps, driving us to admit that 'every motion of matter is simultaneous with some . . . event which might be part of a consciousness'. In a rare and detailed study of Clifford's metaphysics, Mander (2020, 174) explains Clifford's reasoning: if nature makes no jumps, mind-matter correlations must hold below the level at which you get self-aware (e.g. human) consciousness. Furthermore, *all* matter correlates to mind in some way – we have arrived at panpsychism. Clifford claims that every feeling is a 'complex', comprising elements of 'Mind-stuff':

> That element of which . . . even the simplest feeling is a complex, I shall call *Mind-stuff*. A moving molecule of inorganic matter does not possess mind, or consciousness; but it possesses a small piece of mind-stuff. When molecules are so combined together as to form the film on the under side of a jelly-fish, the elements of mind-stuff which go along with them are so combined as to form the faint beginnings of Sentience. . . . When matter takes the complex form of a living human brain, the corresponding mind-stuff takes the form of a human consciousness, having intelligence and volition. (Clifford, 1878, 65)

For Clifford, a human consciousness is a complex with the properties of intelligence and volition, made up of mind-stuff elements which in themselves are not intelligent or wilful. He goes on to explain that matter is not merely correlated with mind-stuff, matter is *identical* with mind-stuff:

> [T]he reality external to our minds which is represented in our minds as matter, is in itself mind-stuff. The universe, then, consists entirely of mind-stuff. (Clifford, 1878, 66)

Our 'imperfect representation' of mind-stuff as matter is what we call the 'material universe'. 'On the Nature of Things-in-Themselves' was reprinted in Clifford's posthumous 1879 *Lectures and Essays*, edited by his friends Frederick Pollock and Leslie Stephen. In his introduction to these volumes, Pollock (1879, 39) notes that as Clifford's ultimate elements are mind, not matter, Clifford's metaphysics must 'be reckoned on the idealist side': 'To speak technically, it is an idealist monism.'[52]

Let's move on to Lloyd Morgan, whose account of the mind changed significantly over the course of his career. Blitz (1992, 59) identifies several phases in his thought, the earliest of which runs from 1882 to 1912. As Welby died in 1912, she did not have the chance to engage with the work he produced during later phases. Lloyd Morgan's 1890 *Animal Life and Intelligence* sets out his early position in especial detail. In the final chapter, 'Mental Evolution', Lloyd Morgan (1890, 465–7) describes two kinds of phenomena. One is physical or physiological phenomena, which include 'neuroses': 'molecular changes in the brain'. Physical phenomena are explained 'in terms of energy', so he labels them 'kinetic'. The other kind of phenomena is mental or conscious, including 'psychoses': 'states of consciousness'. He labels these mental phenomena 'metakinetic'.

Lloyd Morgan argues that neuroses have evolved from 'simpler modes of molecular motion': complex neuroses have evolved from simpler neuroses, and simple neuroses have evolved from non-organic modes of motion. Crucially, psychoses have *also* evolved – from simpler modes of metakinesis: complex psychoses have evolved from simpler psychoses, and simple psychoses have evolved from non-conscious phenomena. Against mind-body dualism, he argues for monism:

> According to the hypothesis that is known as *the monistic hypothesis*, the so-called connection between the molecular changes in the brain and the concomitant states of consciousness is assumed to be identity ... *neurosis is psychosis.* (Lloyd Morgan, 1890, 465)

---

[52] Mander (2020, 176) reaches the same conclusion: 'Clifford's view ... is ultimately a species of *idealism*'.

In other words, kinetic phenomena (molecular brain activity) is identical with the metakinetic (states of consciousness). Lloyd Morgan uses this monism to explain how human consciousness has come about:

> According to the monistic hypothesis, *every mode of kinesis has its concomitant mode of metakinesis, and when the kinetic manifestations assume the form of the molecular processes in the human brain, the metakinetic manifestations assume the form of human consciousness.* ... All matter is not conscious, because consciousness is the metakinetic concomitant of a highly specialized order of kinesis. But every kinesis has an associated metakinesis; and *parallel to the evolution of organic and neural kinesis there has been an evolution of metakinetic manifestations culminating in conscious thought.* (Lloyd Morgan, 1890, 467)

As energy forms '*molecular processes in the human brain*', so also metakinesis forms '*human consciousness*'. Lloyd Morgan (1890, 468) goes on to explain that the kinetic and metakinenetic are 'different phenomenal manifestations of the same noumenal series'. 'Matter' and 'spirit' are 'merged' in a substance which is 'unknown ... in itself'.[53]

Lloyd Morgan intermittently corresponded with Welby from 1888 to 1906; their 1890–1 correspondence is of especial interest to us. In a letter to Welby dated 17 July 1891, Lloyd Morgan sets out the monistic position given here, and describes metakinesis in more detail:

> [Y]ou have the development of consciousness. From what? ... From those lower forms of pre-consciousness-which-is-not-yet-consciousness-but-which-may-develop-into-consciousness! For which I have coined the word metakinesis. My thesis is, EVERY form of energy has its metakinetic aspect but only in certain forms (neurosis) does the metakinesis rise to the level of consciousness.[54]

This is also a kind of panpsychism: every form of energy has a metakinetic aspect and, when that energy attains certain forms, consciousness appears. Interestingly, a portion of this letter was subsequently published verbatim as a short 'Letter to the Editor' in *Nature* on 6 August 1891; see Lloyd Morgan (1891). It is unclear which he authored first: the letter to Welby, or to *Nature*.

Like Stoney, Romanes, Clifford, and Lloyd Morgan, Welby defends the continuity of evolution with regard to mind. For example, in a letter to Lloyd Morgan dated 8 February 1890, Welby describes the evolution of the mind as 'continuous', and adds:

> I want to urge that our ancestry does not end with man or with the animal or with the organic order. We are akin to the dust of the earth and the moisture and

---

[53] For more on the monism Lloyd Morgan held at this point in his career, see Blitz (1992, 67–71).
[54] VWF, 1970–010/010.

'gases' of the air. The shower and the thunder, aye, and the fire-flash are indeed our distant cousins ...

After all it is the same heat, the same water and the same electricity, like the same oxygen and carbonic acid within us, that it is 'outside' in the universe.[55]

For Welby, our evolutionary ancestors include animals, plants, *and* the earth. Everything in the world shares a common nature. The last line of this passage hints at Welby's frustration with theories of the mind that sharply demarcate the 'inner' mind from the 'outer' world, implicitly denying their common nature. Her reading notes of leading psychology books often make this critique. For example, her notes on Harald Hoffding's 1891 *Outlines of Psychology* ask, 'How did the original <u>outside</u> and <u>inside</u> – whether of a body or a nut – become sublimated into indicating the difference between matter and mind?' She adds, '"Mental" life must be drawn without break from "organic" life and this again from "physical" nature.'[56] Similarly, her notes on the very first page of Sully's 1892 *The Human Mind* complain, 'why here and in the following pages insert a superfluous in and out?'.[57]

Welby's view that the evolution of mind is continuous powers her preference for panpsychism. In the same letter to Lloyd Morgan, dated 8 February 1890, she adds:

> I often feel one could accept Prof. Clifford's Mind-stuff if only instead of Stuff he had said Activity; a quiver of Mind–wave or Mind beat! For to me everywhere the ultimate key to the mental – and to the personal – is not matter but Motion, is dynamical and not statical.[58]

For Clifford, every molecule of inorganic matter possesses 'a small piece of mind-stuff'. As molecules increase in complexity, sentience appears. In keeping with her broader metaphysics, Welby is saying she could accept this if the 'stuff' part of Clifford's metaphysics were replaced by 'activity'; this recalls her rejection, given in Section 3.3, of 'stuff and nonsense'. On this position, presumably every individual motion within the dynamic system that is Motion possesses 'Mind-activity', but it is only when motions increase in complexity that sentience appears. I find confirmation of this reading in her later correspondence with Lloyd Morgan.

Having received Lloyd Morgan's 17 July 1891 letter on metakinesis, Welby replies on 25 July 1891. Implicitly accepting the rest of his theory, she writes there is only one 'real difficulty' between us. To explain that difficulty, she quotes Lloyd Morgan, underlining the crucial first word of

---

[55] VWF, 1970–010/010.   [56] VWF, 1970–010/022–08.   [57] VWF, 1970–010/022–08.
[58] VWF, 1970–010/010.

his thesis: 'Every form of energy has its metakinetic aspect but only in certain forms (neurosis) does the metakinesis rise to the level of consciousness.' Of this thesis, Welby writes, 'All I want you to add is, "what we commonly call consciousness".' Otherwise, she explains, 'finality and completeness in our self-analysis creeps in' – we should not assume 'we know all about "consciousness"'. As I read Welby, she fully agrees with Lloyd Morgan that *every* form of energy has its metakinetic aspect, but only in certain forms does it rise to the level of what we know as consciousness. She is allowing for forms of consciousness that we do *not* commonly label as such – for forms of consciousness currently unknown to us.

Further evidence of Welby's openness to other forms of consciousness can be found in a letter she wrote to Norman Pearson on 20 October 1886:

> [Y]ou yourself point out that the primary notion of matter is resistance ... so far from being 'dead' it may well be that 'matter' – resisting force – is living and conscious in some sense which we are not advanced enough as yet to grasp.[59]

This speculation also suggests that Welby's panpsychism preceded her correspondence with Lloyd Morgan. Perhaps her position developed through her earlier study of W. K. Clifford. Lucy Clifford (1924, 102) remembers that, during her 1886 Switzerland trip with Welby, she 'was very eager concerning my husband's views', and 'had a copy of his *Lectures and Essays* with her, the margins already covered with notes'. Given her openness to unknown forms of life and consciousness, Welby would surely have welcomed one of the more unusual observations made in *Electric Movement*. Armstrong (1897a, 49–50) observes that some of his photographs of 'electric delineation on dust' present 'the appearance of organic forms': 'I have already spoken of electricity as organized motion, and we have here an example of it carried apparently to the very verge of life.' For example, Armstrong notes that Figure 2 resembles biological cells, and Figure 3 resembles lichen. The thesis that Motion produces similar forms in both electricity and living creatures must surely have appealed to Welby.

Returning to Lloyd Morgan's theory of metakinesis, in a letter dated 21 September 1891, Welby adds:

> Granting (as I do fully) that metakinesis is inseparable from kinesis though (not absolutely but) practically and relatively distinct; at what point of coarseness do or can we suppose that it develops into psychosis? Supposing that our means of analysing the ultimate constituents of what we call the 'physical' body were a hundred times more delicate and thorough than they are and we re-found the representatives of all the constituent parts of our

---

[59] VWF, 1970–010/012.

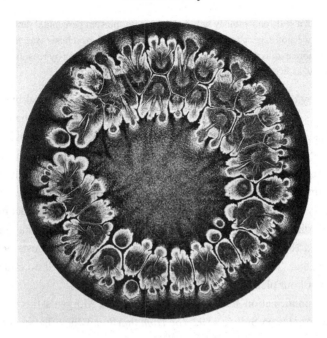

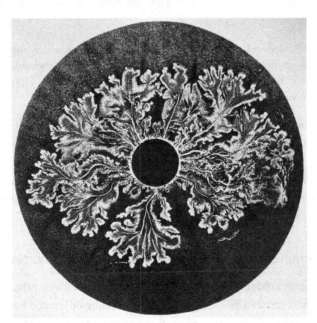

Figure 2 & 3 Electricity resembling living forms. Taken from Armstrong (1899, Plates 38 and 39). These images are in the public domain; they are reproduced from a copy at Ushaw College, Durham, with permission of the Trustees of Ushaw College

> frame on a scale enormously below or above our present perceptual range ...
> should we not expect to find that the accompanying psychosis was just as
> much more exquisitely sensitive? That it had escaped our ken by reason of its
> delicacy, as even the quartz fibres escape the casual eye?[60]

Again, Welby is suggesting here that as we do not know when metakinesis (pre-consciousness) develops into psychosis (states of consciousness), there may be forms of psychosis that as yet we are unaware. Perhaps there is consciousness on a scale 'enormously below' our perceptual range, such as on the scale of quartz fibres, which are measured in microns, one micron being one-thousandth of a millimetre. Alternatively, there may be consciousness on a scale 'enormously ... above' our perceptual range – perhaps one that encompasses a planet or solar systems. Welby's fascination with scale was long-standing. For example, in a 1882–5 letter to Julia Wedgwood, Welby (repr. in Cust, 1929, 98–9) stresses that 'telescopes reveal more and more clearly the comparative minuteness of our planet and scale of life'.

Further confirmation that Welby accepts Lloyd Morgan's theory can be found in her notes on Sully's 1892 *The Human Mind*, which (having critiqued Sully's position) set forth her own view on how our 'primitive' ancestors conceived the world:

> [H]e [our ancestor] resolves it [the world] into motions within motions,
> impulses, energies, forces, of which he is one. And in this he accords with
> the whole bent of recent physics, and with LM's [Lloyd Morgan's]
> metakinesis.[61]

For Welby, our ancestors rightly conceived the world as motions and energies – and included ourselves amongst those motions and energies. In so doing, they anticipated vortex theories of matter, and Lloyd Morgan's metakinesis, on which pre-consciousness 'which-may-develop-into-consciousness' accompanies every form of energy. This thesis, that pre-consciousness or mind-activity pervades the universe, confirms Welby's idealism.

6.2 Complicating Welby's Panpsychism: Novelty in Nature

Although Welby holds a panpsychism akin to that defended by Clifford in 1878, and Lloyd Morgan in 1890, I argue there is a major difference between her position and theirs: Welby takes phenomena such as mind or consciousness to be really 'new' or novel. This difference emerges most clearly when we ask how many kinds of being there. As Blitz (1992, 56) explains, many evolutionists

---

[60] VWF, 1970–010/010. A version of this letter is published in Cust (1929, 275–7).
[61] VWF, 1970–010/022–08.

who accepted the continuity of evolution defended some form of monism, on which there is just one kind of being. Monism was popular amongst the thinkers Welby engaged with. Clifford's mind-stuff offers a kind of monism. Drawing on the work of his late friend Clifford, Romanes (1885, 88–9) identifies mind with motion, arguing against 'seeming duality'. In 1895, Lloyd Morgan edited a collection of Romanes' posthumous essays, titling it *Mind and Motion and Monism*. On Lloyd Morgan's 1890 system there is also only one kind of substance, of unknown nature; Blitz (1992, 56) notes that Lloyd Morgan's monism draws on that of Romanes.

In contrast, Welby rejects monism. In a letter to Hodgson dated 10 October 1890, Welby writes that she prefers a kind of 'Triunism' over 'Dualism and even Monism'.[62] On her triunism, 'the conception of Matter as the supreme Premiss' is 'replaced by that of Motion'. Presumably, the remaining, non-supreme elements of her triune would be matter and mind. (Hodgson dryly replies on 13 October 1890: 'I cannot help being a little amused at your own "supreme Premiss – Motion" ... Thomson only gets as far as Vortex.'[63]) Furthermore, in her unpublished essay, 'A Significant Question', dated 1903, Welby writes:

> [C]hange of degree will issue in change of kind. And here lies the secret of 'matter and mind'. They must not be confounded: they are two 'different' products of ... 'Motion'.[64]

One element of this passage is familiar: Welby is arguing that Motion produces matter and mind. Another element is unfamiliar: Welby is arguing that matter and mind are 'different', and that their 'secret' lies in how 'change of degree will issue in change of kind'. This unfamiliar element is important. Unfortunately, Welby does not explain her thesis that change of degree issues in change of kind, but I argue we should understand it as follows. I will set out my reading of Welby's position, and contextualise the position I ascribe to her, before offering some texts that support it.

At the core of my reading is the idea that Welby was attempting to allow for genuine newness within her metaphysics. In the above passage, I read Welby as holding that changes in degrees of *motion* result in change of kind. When motion changes to one degree, it results in a new kind of being, matter; when it changes to another degree, it results in another new kind of being, mind. Similarly, you might hold that, as water changes in degree (becoming colder or hotter) it changes in kind (becoming ice, liquid, steam). It is always water, just

---

[62] VWF, 1970–010/007–01.

[63] VWF, 1970–010/007–01. A version of this letter is published in Cust (1929, 259).

[64] VWF, 1970–010/031–10.

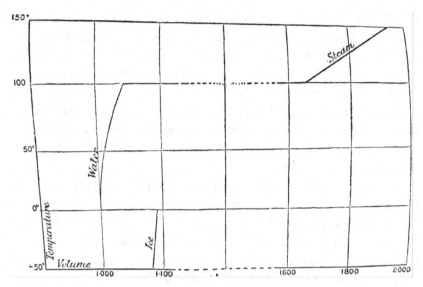

Figure 4 Illustrating 'breaches of continuity in development' through the production of ice, water, and steam. Taken from Lloyd Morgan (1894, 335). This image is in the public domain; it is reproduced (with permission) from a copy in private ownership

as we are always Motion; yet small, incremental changes produce new kinds of being. To illustrate this idea, consider Figure 4. This 1894 graph charts the volume to temperature relationship for water in each of its three states, indicating breaks at the freezing and boiling points. On my reading, changes in degrees of motion produce analogous 'breaks' in Welby's continuous world: at each break, a new, higher level phenomena appears. To better understand this, it will be helpful to compare my reading of Welby's system with another system that also posits levels within reality: that of Samuel Alexander's 1920 *Space, Time, and Deity.*

Figure 5 illustrates the levels within Alexander's metaphysics.[65] At the bottom level is 'Motion', Alexander's (1920, vol. 1, 61) label for 'Space-Time', 'a system of motions'. Alexander (1920, vol. 1, xi) describes Motion as the 'stuff of the world'. On his system, the whole universe comprises Motion, but it is only on the lowest level of reality that we find 'pure Motion, before matter has been generated in it'. As indicated by the arrow in Figure 5, Alexander's levels increase in complexity from bottom to top: pure Motion, the least complex, produces the increasingly complex matter, life, and mind. The narrowing of the pyramid from base to apex indicates

---

[65] This representation of Alexander's system is adapted from Lloyd Morgan (1927, 11), who describes it as 'pyramidal'. The original diagram is in the public domain.

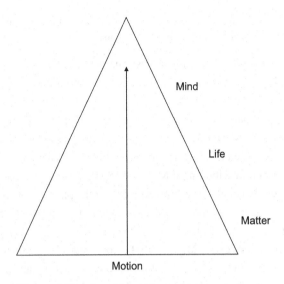

Figure 5 Levels within Alexander's metaphysics

relative scarcity of phenomena: the universe exhibits less life than matter, and even less mind.

There is a striking similarity between the metaphysics of Welby and Alexander: both place 'Motion' at the heart of their systems, and claim that Motion produces matter and mind. I do not wish to overstate this similarity: Alexander's unique metaphysic of Motion differs in many ways from that of Welby.[66] Yet, given this shared thesis, Alexander's system makes an excellent foil for Welby's. An instructive difference between them lies in *how* Alexander conceives new phenomena to appear at different levels within Motion: via the mechanism of 'emergence'. It will be instructive to give a brief history of emergentism.

Let's say you are an evolutionist who wishes to affirm the continuity of evolution with regard to mind, and avoid positing supernatural interventions; *and* allow that 'mind' or 'consciousness' is a genuinely novel phenomena, something that is found in human beings but not in rocks. Effectively, you are seeking a way out of Wallace's dilemma. Blitz's study of the development of evolutionary emergentism argues that, over the course of his career, Lloyd Morgan sought precisely that:

> Was it possible to combine full recognition of qualitative novelty, particularly as concerned life and mind – as Wallace did – without rejecting the continuity of the evolutionary process and its naturalistic framework – as required by

---

[66] On Alexander's work more generally, see Thomas (2022).

Darwin? This was the basic problem that Lloyd Morgan faced in his development of emergent evolution. (Blitz, 1992, 56)

Blitz (1992, 59–61) describes the earliest phase of Lloyd Morgan's career as 'pre-emergentist'. Figure 4 is actually taken from another of Lloyd Morgan's pre-emergentist books, his 1894 *Introduction to Comparative Psychology*. Here, Blitz argues that Lloyd Morgan came close to admitting that 'something new' could occur in evolution, just as during changes in state of water, but such phenomena 'introduced a difficulty' for his belief in Darwinian continuity. Of such breaches of continuity, Lloyd Morgan (1894, 338) wrote, 'There does *not* appear to be a gradual and insensible change from the physical properties of the elements to the physical properties of the compound . . . at the critical moment of the constitution of the compound there seems to be a *new departure*' (my emphasis). Perhaps Lloyd Morgan felt he had ceded too much ground to thinkers such as Wallace, who posited genuine novelties in nature because, in the second edition of *An Introduction to Comparative Psychology*, he added a new paragraph:

> At the same time it should be clearly grasped that these apparent breaches of continuity are to be regarded as merely incidental. . . . Could we . . . find the appropriate conditions, every apparent breach of continuity would probably disappear. We are constrained to believe that evolution as a process is essentially one and continuous. (Lloyd Morgan, 1903, 359)

The problem is that, in the absence of further argument, Lloyd Morgan's description of these breaches as 'apparent' and 'merely incidental' is unconvincing.

Blitz (1992, 59) explains that during the middle phase of his career, from 1912 to 1915, Lloyd Morgan developed a theory of emergentism; from 1915 onwards until his death, he systematically defended that theory.[67] On Blitz's reading, it took Lloyd Morgan many years to develop emergentism because the process required synthesising several independent philosophical ideas. Of his later writings, Lloyd Morgan's 1927 *Emergent Evolution* is especially comprehensive. In its opening pages, Lloyd Morgan (1927, 1–2) writes that when we consider the history of the world, we occasionally find 'something genuinely new', such as 'the advent of life', 'mind', and 'reflective thought'. Contra the supernaturalists, he aims to treat these novelties 'without invoking any extranatural Power'. The mechanism of emergence allowed Lloyd Morgan and Alexander to escape Wallace's dilemma. They claimed that, as matter becomes increasingly complex, genuinely novel properties can 'emerge', attaining

---

[67] Lloyd Morgan was the first to develop emergentism, but Alexander was the first to publish on it, in *Space, Time, and Deity*. The two men were friends, and Alexander credited Lloyd Morgan with priority; see Blitz (1992, 103).

a higher ontological level. Thus, novelties such as mind can emerge in nature without recourse to supernatural intervention.

To illustrate emergentism further, let's return to Alexander. *Space, Time, and Deity* claims that, as motions become increasingly complex, new qualities *emerge*, resulting in the hierarchy of levels. In this way, Matter emerges from pure Motion, life emerges from matter, and mind emerges from life:

> Empirical things or existents are ... groupings within Space-Time, that is, they are complexes of ... motions in various degrees of complexity ... as in the course of Time new complexity of motions comes into existence, a new quality emerges ... [For example] the emergence of the quality of consciousness from a lower level of complexity which is vital [alive].
>
> (Alexander, 1920, vol. 2, 45)

On my reading of Welby, she holds many of the claims made here. Material bodies *are* complexes of motions and, as motions become more complex, *new* qualities such as life and consciousness appear, attaining higher levels within reality.

Having set out this reading, I offer some textual evidence in support of it. In a few letters, Welby seems to conceive matter, life, and mind as 'ascending' levels in nature. Consider this 1885–6 letter to mathematician Mary Everest Boole:

> There is no 'break' or 'gulf' anywhere, as the scientists are beginning to discover. What we need is the principle of levelling up. Upward and expanding tendency is the very essence of what I suppose Darwin's truth to mean; so the lowest contains the elements of the highest in the order of ascension. (Welby, repr. in Cust, 1929, 154)

I take this to mean that evolution exhibits no breaks, but we still need a 'principle of levelling up': a mechanism to explain the upward tendency within nature.

Next, consider this 1888–90 letter to McClure:

> [O]n my line, 'mind' is nothing but a new way or path – method – of development, a new mode of motion, a new means of bringing about change; just as the organic [i.e. living beings] is but a new complex of the motions we find throughout in the inorganic [i.e. non-living beings], whether as physical or chemical. (Welby, repr. in Cust, 1929, 214)

Here, Welby seems to be describing three levels: (i) the 'inorganic', including physical or chemical elements; (ii) the 'organic', which presumably includes plants and less-than-sentient animals; and (iii) 'mind'. At each level, she writes that something *new* appears: the organic is 'a new complex of the motions' that we find in the inorganic, just as mind, 'a new way', is a new complex of the motions that we find in the organic. She returns to (what appear to be the same) three levels in a letter to Norman Pearson, dated 4 February 1890. Having urged Pearson not to stop using the ideas of 'soul' and 'spirit', just because they were used in pre-scientific contexts, Welby adds:

> As to soul and spirit do not let us lightly lose . . . distinctions which may well prove to be more than ever needed in illuminating metaphor. Take three levels in the organic world, [(i)] organic structure, which persists at least for a short – and as mummified for a long – while, when 'life' has fled; then [(ii)] that life itself, and [(iii)] thirdly consciousness. You have roughly body, soul, and spirit as at least a figure – whether the ultimately best or not – of a broadly threefold order.[68]

Putting these texts together, I depict Welby's account of reality in Figure 6; to stress the similarities I perceive between her system and Alexander's, I also use a pyramidal scheme.[69] On Figure 6, Motion gives rise to matter, matter gives rise to the organic, and the organic gives rise to mind. As Stone (forthcoming) explains, Welby argued that Darwin's *Descent of Man* was inappropriately titled – for

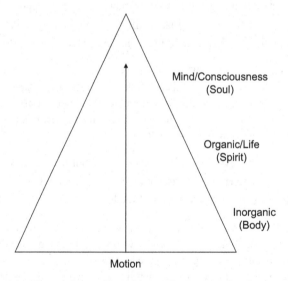

Figure 6 Levels within Welby's metaphysics

[68] VWF, 1970–010/012.
[69] Following from her dynamic conception of the world as Motion, Welby famously disliked metaphors involving 'substances', 'foundations', and 'bases'; see Stone (forthcoming). Given this, she would probably dislike seeing her system represented as a pyramid with Motion at its base. As Welby sometimes expresses the relationship between levels of nature using metaphors of containment, perhaps she would prefer to see her system represented as a series of concentric circles on which Motion, the largest circle, contains successively smaller ones.

Darwin's aim was to document the *ascent* of man: 'how humanity has *emerged from* lower animals rather than *regressed back* into their condition'.

This brings us to my final piece of textual evidence: Welby's notes on Hoffding's *Outlines of Psychology*. In this book, Hoffding (1891, 36–7) argues that 'the plant' and 'the animal' are different 'types of life'. One difference between them is that, unlike the animal, the plant 'uses up its energies wholly in the life of nutrition', such as in growing. Nature prepares everything for it. In this regard, he claims that 'the plant is like a foetus, it remains in the maternal bosom of nature, and has not made its way out to independent, individual life'. Welby's notes reject Hoffding's position, arguing there must be continuity between all types of life:

> 'Mental' life must be drawn without break from 'organic' life and this again from 'physical' nature. . . .
>
> Take now Prof. Hoffding's comparison. Reverse it. Perhaps the foetus-life is really like plant life, that is, the two have a common germ and mode of growth and the animal is really a born plant, a freed vegetative organism. Then, when what we call mind or intelligence comes in, we have as kinetic what has throughout been potential or stored up: mind is the katabolic moment, the explosive crisis of a long anabolic process.[70]

Against Hoffding, Welby claims the foetus is really like a plant: plant and animal life share 'a common germ', implying there is no 'break' between them. And yet, despite this continuity between plant and animal life, there is still a point where mind 'comes in'. Importantly, this passage suggests a *mechanism* for the arrival of mind.

I do not find evidence that Welby explains the arrival of mind using emergence. In fact, I read this passage as offering an *alternative* to emergentism, via anabolic and catabolic processes. The anabolic process involves creating bigger, complex molecules from smaller, simpler molecules. In contrast, the catabolic process involves breaking down complex molecules, releasing energy for a body to use. Welby's speculation seems to be that plants and human foetuses grow in the same way, except that in the foetus the anabolic process leads to a catabolic explosion, releasing energy that manifests as mind. To my mind, the details of this mechanism are unimportant – what matters is that she felt the need to *offer* one, to explain the arrival of novel phenomena within nature. I take this as evidence that Welby was also searching for a way out of Wallace's dilemma. One part of her solution, that new phenomena appear on different levels of nature, is akin to the mature work of emergentists Lloyd Morgan and Alexander. Another part of her solution, that

---

[70] VWF, 1970–010/022–08.

these new phenomena appear via anabolic-catabolic processes, differs from those emergentists: they are using different mechanisms to explain how those new phenomena appear.

Welby is a panpsychist, positing 'mind-activity' or metakinesis throughout nature. Yet, in my view, her panpsychism is complicated by her assertion that matter, life, and mind, are new phenomena. This leads her to reject the monism defended by panpsychists such as Clifford, Romanes, and Lloyd Morgan, in favour of a triune, levelled account of reality. Of course, these two theses are in tension. How can you hold that mind-activity floods the universe, an activity that is somehow continuous with mind; *and* that mind is a novelty only occurring on higher levels of reality? On my reading, Welby would respond as follows. Mind-activity is everywhere, yet mind-activity is merely a kind of pre-consciousness; only in rare forms, such as human beings, does it develop into sentience, and these forms represent breaks within the world. These 'breaks' are novel, yet not discontinuous with the rest of nature. Although plausible, this answer does not remove the tension altogether. Just as Lloyd Morgan struggled for years towards his theory of emergence, I read Welby as struggling towards her own account of mind.

6.3 Networking with Metaphysicians of Mind

The final part of this section reflects on the personal connections between Welby and some of the metaphysically minded thinkers named earlier in this Element. We have already seen that she was in touch with many people important to the late W. K. Clifford, including his wife Lucy, and his friends Romanes, Pollock, and Stephens. Welby may have met this circle through Lucy Clifford, who was well known for hosting salons: her regular visitors included Pollock and Stephens.[71] Lucy Clifford (1924, 102) remembers that, in 1886 Switzerland, Welby 'asked ... about many who were my friends'. Here, I show that Welby used her network to bring metaphysicians of mind together.

To give a pertinent example, on 2 December 1891 Welby invited Lodge to visit her at Easter, 'in order to meet & compare notes with one or two other thinkers who like you are sounding the depths of life from the physical side'. She adds that other possible guests include Lloyd Morgan, Sully, Hodgson, and Romanes. Notably, all these thinkers had published on the nature of the mind, and its place in nature. On 7 December, Lodge accepted her invitation.[72] Welby's Easter plans are soon afoot. In a letter to Hodgson dated 31 December 1891, Welby invites him to what has become a five-day 'little gathering':

---

[71] See Demoor (2004).   [72] VWF, 1970–010/009.

Its object is the informal discussion of the remoter or more indirect implications of present scientific research, & of the 'borderlands' which at present are so difficult to explore & even to recognise. ... The following have definitely accepted: Profs. P. Geddes, Lloyd Morgan, Ray Lancaster, C.V. Boys; Dr. Romanes, Dr. O. Lodge, Mr. J Sully, Mr. F. Galton (if in England then) and Mr. A. Balfour – Also Mr. Titchener from Wundt's Laboratory.

... Will you not let us persuade you for once to break your seclusion and join us? I need not say how real & warm would be the pleasure it would give me. And of course there will only be easy and informal intercourse, with the advantage of a large quiet house and plenty of light, air & warmth. Prof. Lloyd Morgan is especially anxious for the honour of knowing you being a strong admirer of your Philosophy.[73]

On 4 January 1892, Hodgson accepted her invitation: 'The detachment of lieges whom you have summoned is indeed a brilliant one . . . [an] intellectual feast.' As best I can tell, this visit went ahead: on this and presumably many other occasions, Welby hosted a philosophical salon.

This gathering is of especial interest because it involves so many thinkers who wrote on the mind. Also note that Welby's correspondence with Lloyd Morgan on panpsychism, set out in Section 6.1, took place just a few months earlier – from July to September 1891. Given this, it seems likely that Lloyd Morgan and Welby would have discussed the mind further at Denton, and I wonder whether, or how, their relationship affected the development of their views. We have seen that Welby agreed with much of Lloyd Morgan's position, and there is evidence that Lloyd Morgan drew on her thought in at least one area. In a letter to Welby dated 12 July 1905, Schiller describes overhearing Lloyd Morgan give a talk using some of her phraseology and ideas: 'I sat next to him at dinner afterwards & taxed him with it whereupon he owned up.'[74] Of the synthesis that would eventually become Lloyd Morgan's emergentism, Blitz (1992, 88–90) claims that a key idea is that reality possesses strata, or levels; he argues that Lloyd Morgan borrowed this idea from Walter T. Marvin's 1912 metaphysics. Welby does not appear anywhere in Blitz's study of Lloyd Morgan's development but I wonder if he might also have garnered this idea from her.

Although Welby did not make contact with Alexander until after Easter 1892 – her introductory letter is dated 16 May 1892 – they also corresponded, intermittently but at length, until 1911. I have not found any letters discussing Motion but they evidently met several times, raising the possibility they shared ideas about this element of their metaphysics in person. Charmingly, in a letter

---

[73] VWF, 1970–010/007–02.   [74] VWF, 1970–010/014–08.

dated 22 June 1908, Welby writes to Alexander of his impending visit: 'I defy you to bore me! Duneaves shall be fortified.'[75]

7 Time

7.1 Introducing Welby's Work on Time

Welby's writings on time span her career. They include an essay 'The Now', published in her first 1881 book *Links and Clues*; correspondence and unpublished essays from the 1880s onwards; and two papers in *Mind*, her 1907 'Time as Derivative', and 1909 'Mr. McTaggart on the "Unreality of Time"'. Of these texts, 'Time as Derivative' is particularly important: at seventeen dense pages, it constitutes Welby's lengthiest engagement with time; and, as I have so far discovered eleven drafts of the paper, she clearly cared deeply about its contents. As its title indicates, the paper argues that time is a derivative phenomenon. More specifically, that time derives from space.

Unlike the other topics considered in this study, Welby's account of time, chiefly as presented in 'Time as Derivative', has been studied extensively.[76] Yet, with the exception of my own work, the literature implies that Welby's account of time is primarily concerned with language. For example, scholars have described 'Time as Derivative' as an 'application of signific maxims' to time, and as focused on 'issues of interpretation'.[77] In their detailed studies of Welby on time, Petrilli (2009, 388–403) and Luisi (2013) also give this impression, partly because both consider Welby's position, and 'Time as Derivative', through Welby's 1903–11 language-focused correspondence with Peirce. Against this trend, I have argued (Thomas, forthcoming b) that 'Time as Derivative' is primarily concerned with metaphysics – as advancing a theory of what time *is*.

This section builds on my earlier work, chronologically exploring the development of Welby's views on time, further detailing my reading of her mature metaphysic, and placing that account within her broader system. As I read Welby, her early work only advances an account of the *features* of time, holding for example that all events or times comprise a co-existing whole. As her career progresses, she develops an additional, complementary position on

---

[75] VWF, 1970–010/001–06.

[76] There are three sustained studies of Welby on time: Petrilli (2009, 388–403), Luisi (2013), and Thomas (forthcoming b). Shorter discussions can also be found in Schmitz (1985, lxix), Myers (1995, 19), and Ingthorsson (2016, 64, 79–80). Myers (1995, 19) describes Welby's research on time as 'brief', a mere 'excursion' within her thought. As this section should evidence, such characterisations are inaccurate.

[77] See Eschbach (1983, xiii) and Myers (1995, 17).

the *nature* of time: that time is a kind of space. This position emerges full-blown in 'Time as Derivative' and, I argue, it constitutes an anti-realism about time.

7.2 Welby's Block Universe (1881 Onwards)

As I read Welby, she ascribes certain *features* to time across almost her entire career. First, all times or events comprise a co-existing whole. Second, nothing is really past, present, or future. Third, the time series is *multi-directional*, permitting movement in multiple directions: although we usually think that times or events run from past to future, they may also run from future to past. The first two features commit Welby to a 'block universe'. Barry Dainton (2010, 7–9) describes such a universe as follows: 'all moments of time (and all events) are equally real ... differences between past, present and future are simply differences of perspective'. He compares block universes with solid chunks of marble, explaining that 'the dynamic features of the universe, such as change and movement', are 'patterns running along the block'. Although block universe theories need not take time to be multi-directional, they often do, perhaps partly because of H. G. Wells' infamous novel *The Time Machine*, which describes a time traveller moving backwards and forwards through time within a block universe.

Block universe theories were common in the late nineteenth century, and the term itself dates to 1880s.[78] For example, F. H. Bradley (1883, 53) describes a view on which 'the past and future stretches in a block behind us and before us'. William James (1884, 223) complains that certain views around timelessness are 'just another way of whacking upon us the block-universe'. Drawing on Hegel, J. M. E. McTaggart (1894, 192) defended a block universe theory: 'reality is one timeless whole, in which all that appears successive is really co-existent, as the houses are coexistent which we see successively from the windows of a train'.

I read Welby as describing the features of time in (what I believe to be) her earliest writing on the subject, her 1881 essay 'The "Now"':

> Let us try the effect of putting ourselves into the 'Now' of God for a moment, and out of our own earthly past, present, and future, into eternity; out of the 'has been and shall be' into the IS ... Let us thus try to get a fresh view of all the great cardinal truths ... we shall get *dimly* a glimpse of eternal Fact: the changeless, the solid, the immovable; we are freed for an instant from the necessary bondage alike of passing event or of passing thought, and reach ... to the verge of that which IS; and which, essentially *being*, must 'for ever' have

---

[78] I owe this to Nahin's (2017, 94–5) study, which finds that the term 'block universe' evolves through Hegel, James, and Bradley.

been, and 'for ever' continue. Only for moments can any soul thus penetrate here the time-veil . . . [we are] fettered by time barrier. (Welby, 1881, 196–7)

From our earthly perspective, events are future, present, or past. Yet from God's perspective, nothing is past, present, and future; everything is 'changeless', 'solid', and 'immoveable' – it simply 'is'. God sees the world as it truly is, whilst we are usually prevented from seeing this by a 'time-veil' or 'time barrier'. This passage describes events as co-existing, for all events exist changelessly; and it claims that nothing is really past, present, or future. Welby's universe is a block.

New content added to the second, 1883 edition of *Links and Clues* confirms this reading. In support of her claim that we are fettered by a time barrier, Welby (1883, 158) quotes Augustine: we 'fluttereth between the motions of things past and to come', while 'in the Eternal nothing passeth, but the whole is present'. Furthermore, she references a new, 1880 edition of Felix Eberty's *The Stars and the Earth: Or, Thoughts Upon Space, Time, and Eternity.*[79] Welby (1883, 156) writes that this book 'brings out with singular force the purely relative value of conditions of space and time . . . we are able easily to conceive changes in the present physical order of things, or rather in the point of view from which we regard them, which would entirely revolutionise our apparently most necessary notions of "past, present, future"'. In the book, Eberty (1880, 7) explains that light takes time to travel: we don't see the moon as it is, but as it was about a second before. Depending on where we are, we can see places as they were at various times. Thus, he reasons, the events on earth of eight minutes ago can be seen from the sun, whilst the events on earth of 4,000 years ago can be seen from a faraway star. Eberty (1880, 11–12) argues this allows us to understand God's omniscience via his omnipresence: 'if we imagine the eye of God present at every point of space', the world's whole history 'is at the present moment actually extended in space'. Welby doesn't explain why she takes *The Stars and the Earth* to 'revolutionise' our 'apparently' necessary notions of past, present, and future. But presumably her reasoning is something like this: if the same event can be witnessed at different times from different points in space, it makes little sense to speak of that event as being past, present, or future. As on God's perspective, each event simply is.

Evidence that Welby ascribes multi-directionality to time can be found a few years later, in her anonymously published 1885 dialogue, 'An Echo of Larger Life'. Perhaps it was written with Eberty in mind, for the narrator recounts

---

[79] Eberty's book was first published anonymously in 1846, and ran through many editions and translations; notably, the 1923 edition included an introduction by Einstein. Welby references a newly published, 1880 English-language edition edited by Richard Proctor.

meeting a wise man who showed people 'that their thought could travel in one instant to a distant star and over long ages of time'. The dialogue goes on to explain that those people:

> found that the earth was not flat but a sphere . . . [and realised] that 'up and down' – above and below – were reversed to those at the 'antipodes', and therefore had no real existence in space. (Welby, repr. in Petrilli, 2009, 326)

To a person in London, 'upwards' refers to one direction. To a person at London's antipode (i.e. its geographically opposite part of the planet) in the Pacific Ocean, 'upwards' refers to the reverse direction – to what is, from London's perspective, 'downwards'. Hence 'upwards' and 'downwards' have 'no real existence in space': they are relative to a person's location. Eventually, the same people also discovered:

> that 'past and future' were as purely relative to them as 'upwards and downwards'. . . . the same truth . . . applied to time; that there might well be an 'antipodes' in that sphere too, where past and future were reversed. (Welby, repr. in Petrilli, 2009, 326)

Welby is arguing that to a person at Time 1, 'past' refers to one direction; to a person at Time 2, 'past' refers to the reverse direction – to what is, from Time 1's perspective, 'future'. Time is multi-directional: it is a matter of perspective whether the time series runs past–future or future–past. This thesis anticipates a position advanced in Bradley's 1893 *Appearance and Reality*, which considers our assumption that the time series has a single direction, from past to future. Against this assumption, Bradley (1893, 214) argues that 'the direction, and the distinction between past and future, entirely depends upon *our* experience'.

Two years later, in a letter to Pollock dated 3–4 December 1887, Welby describes her position that all times are a co-existing whole in a different way:

> I wish someone would do for time what the author of Flatland does for space, and tell us of creatures with memory and sense of the present, but no foresight whatever, or with present and future clear to them, but no memory at all, or, again, conscious of the present moment only . . . I suspect . . . that much of our thought, philosophical or theological or other, is still but two-dimensional, and most of it not even binocular but only monocular.[80]

This passage uses two related metaphors to make its point about time. One concerns *Flatland*: Welby is arguing that, like two-dimensional Flatlanders, we do not see the world as it really is. If we could see in a higher number of

---

[80] VWF, 1970–010/013. A version of this letter is published in Cust (1929, 197–8).

dimensions, we would see the past, present, *and* future together – we would see all times as a co-existing whole. The other metaphor concerns binocular vision. Animals with binocular vision, such as humans, integrate different information from two eyes to achieve depth of visual perception. In an 1887 manuscript on mental biology, Welby (repr. in Petrilli, 2009, 470–1) gives a technical explanation of binocular vision, then asks what would happen if mental development should follow physical vision 'and become *biune*' (i.e. two in one). She answers that using a 'binocular' faculty, our intellects could 'detect' third dimensions beyond the usual alternatives of discussion, giving us 'a real depth of insight answering to depths of space . . . a thought-cube, instead of only points, lines, or plane surface-views'. If our mental vision became binocular, we could achieve more insight into the world – and, by implication, one insight would be that we live in a block universe.

In an unpublished essay 'The Significs of Space and Time', dated 9 August 1910, Welby suggests how one might visually represent her universe: 'Let a circle symbolise space and let a row of dots in it represent, as a whole, Time; each dot representing a section or "spot" in Time, which does not "pass"; we "pass" our "time" in or on this or that way or path.'[81] I illustrate this prose description in Figure 7. Again, Welby is straightforwardly describing a block universe.

Before moving on, I add a note on Motion. As I read Welby, she finds 'motion everywhere, motions underlying every phenomenon'. What we usually think of as the material universe *is* 'Motion', the dynamic system containing all smaller motions. Given this, Welby's block universe theory is a theory about Motion. In other words, Motion *is* the block. Like an unchanging block of marble, Motion itself does not change, yet the striations or waves it contains comprise all the changes and movements of the universe. On this reading, Welby's metaphysic of Motion once again prefigures that of Alexander's *Space, Time, and Deity*. As explained in Section 6.2, Alexander (1920, vol. 1, 61–2) also conceives the universe as 'a system of motions . . . a single vast entity Motion'. He is explicit that this universe is a block. To illustrate, Alexander (1920, vol. 1, 64) explains that, on his universe, all the life stages of a 'growing organism' co-exist: its adolescence, maturity, and deterioration. Yet, because it contains all motion within itself, Alexander (1920, vol. 1, 64) describes Motion 'as the theatre of perpetual movement'.[82] Welby and Alexander both place a huge stress on dynamism *within* their block universes.

---

[81] VWF, 1970–010/032–02.

[82] For more on Alexander's block universe, see Thomas (2019, §3).

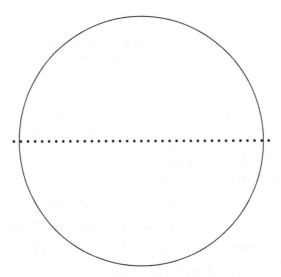

Figure 7 Time within Welby's block universe

7.3 Arriving at the Derivation of Time from Space (circa 1897)

Gradually, alongside Welby's career-long views on the features of time, she also develops a new view regarding the *nature* of time: that it derives from space. This is the position she will eventually defend at length in 'Time as Derivative'. Hints of this view appear in her late 1890s writings, and I have found that Welby herself acknowledges she was developing new ideas during this period. On a set of reading notes, Welby states, 'Written in 1891, about 6 years before I discovered that time had no vocabulary.'[83] As we will see, the thesis that time lacks a vocabulary of its own comprises a key premise in 'Time Is Derivative', so it seems likely that this 1897 realisation played a significant part in Welby's decision to write the paper.

What prompted Welby's 'discovery' that time has no vocabulary? She does not say, but I suggest it stemmed from her reflections on time–space parallelism. Welby's unpublished papers include at least five copies of a table taken from Francis Bowen's historical study, *Modern Philosophy*.[84] Drawing on the work of Arthur Schopenhauer, Bowen's (1877, 179–81) table provides twenty-eight theses or parallels, showing 'the curious parallelism and symmetry which exist between our notions of Space and Time'. To give a flavour of these parallels, I provide the first three:

---

[83] Manuscript headed 'Notes on Prof. Hoffding's "Outlines of Psychology"'; see VWF, 1970–010/022–08.

[84] VWF, 1970–010/032–05.

TIME	SPACE
1. There is but one Time, and all different times are parts of this one	1. The same
2. Different times are not co-existent or simultaneous, but successive	2. Different spaces are not successive, but are co-existent or simultaneous
3. Time cannot be thought away, but everything in Time can be thought away, or imagined as non-existent	3. The same

Welby's papers *also* include several copies of an alternative version of the table – authored by her. One copy is headed '1897-1900', and titled "Paraphrase of a parallel definition of Time + Space (here reversed)". Here, Welby gives her own twenty-eight parallels. Again, the first three provide a flavour:

SPACE	TIME
1. There is but one Space, and all different spaces are parts of this one	1. So in that motion-space which we call Time
2. Different spaces (places, or we contradict prop.1) are successive in relation to Motion, which our defect compels us to spell out letter by letter, pace out step by step; but which like a chord in music is ultimately co-existent or simultaneous	2. Different times (time sections, divisions) are due to our motion-blindness, itself due to our mode of measurement which excludes one time unit while dealing with another so that we are unable to experience time as we can experience space in more than one direction
3. Space cannot be thought away, it can only be translated; but everything in space can be thought away (?)	3. Time is Space translated and can only in this sense be thought away. Again (?)

Parallel (1) asserts the unity of space, and of that particular kind of space *which we call* Time – already hinting at the derivative nature of time. Parallel (2) asserts that the parts of space are co-existent; so too are the parts of time, which we would see if we did not suffer from a kind of blindness with regard to time (more on this blindness in Section 7.4). The question marks next to (3) show that Welby is still working through her ideas of space and time; but it is significant that, already, she states here that 'Time is Space translated'. It seems likely that

Welby's reversal of Bowen's table, reasoning from space *to* time, represents a significant advance towards the development of her mature view. As she claims to have realised that time lacks a vocabulary around 1897, and this table is dated 1897–1900, the timing would certainly fit.

A few years later, Welby began work on 'Time as Derivative'. As best I can tell, she began planning the paper in 1901. In a letter to her assistant R. Greentree dated 31 August 1901, Welby writes that Pollock 'was much interested in my "time" ideas'. In a letter to Schiller dated 22 September 1901, Welby writes, 'I have somewhat developed the ideas of time.' By 11 December 1901, she tells Schiller that she plans to treat the subject 'separately' (i.e. in a stand-alone piece).[85] Of the eleven drafts I have found of this paper, what appears to be the earliest lies in an envelope labelled 'TIME Paper 1902'.[86] This aligns with the fact a draft of the paper was circulating in 1902. Welby *may* have sent a copy to George Stout: in a letter dated 6 January 1902, Welby writes, 'I can't help hoping that, though you could not adopt my view of space and time, you will allow that it is worth advancing?'.[87] She certainly sent a draft to Scottish philosopher W. R. Sorley for, in a letter dated 23 October 1902, he explicitly comments on it.[88] Although the structure of the paper, and the figures it engages with, changes across these drafts, I have found that its core theses remain consistent.

7.4 Welby's Anti-Realist Metaphysic of Time (1900s)

Welby's mature views on the nature of time appear full-blown in her 1907 'Time as Derivative'. I read this paper as advancing a unique kind of anti-realism about time. To make this case, it will be helpful to give an overview of the paper. I distinguish (and label) five sections within it. §I (p. 383) comprises an introduction. §II (pp. 383–5) argues that our language, and ideas, of time derive from space. §III (pp. 385–93) discusses excerpts about time taken from recent literature. Welby argues that some of these excerpts misconceive time, whilst others implicitly support her view. §IV (pp. 393–9) considers the origin of our idea of time, and offers a new metaphysic. The conclusion, §V (pp. 399–400), summarises some of her points. My reading of Welby centres on §IV, but I will say a little about the other sections too.

The opening lines of §I state:

---

[85] VWF, 1970–010/014–06.   [86] VWF, 1970–010/032–03.
[87] VWF, 1970–010/015–23. A version of this letter is published in Cust (1931, 131).
[88] VWF, 1970–010/015.

> THE idea of Time is always found bracketed with that of Space. . . . With rare
> exceptions the two seem to be treated by thinkers of all schools as equally
> original and originative categories . . .
>
>   I venture to suggest that whereas Space is . . . primary . . . Time is the
> product of our experience of Motion and its condition, Space. It is in other
> words a translated application of these two really original ideas.
>
> (Welby, 1907, 383)

We should not 'bracket' space and time (i.e. treat them in parallel) for they are *not*
equal categories. Space is primary, whilst time is not. Time is produced by our
experience of Motion and Space. The rest of the paper expands on these ideas.

In §II, Welby (1907, 383–4) claims that we 'speak of' feelings and ideas as
'following each other' in time, yet 'to follow is a space-motion idea'. Similarly,
we 'speak of vast periods', or a 'short space' of time – 'all spatial ideas'. Time
has 'length'; we can speak of a 'space of time but not of a time of space'. Welby
stresses that her argument does not rely 'wholly' upon the etymology of single
words, but instead on:

> widespread habits of speech leading, in the most diverse languages, to
> a multitude of varying forms which all involve expressing the idea of Time
> by a spatial term . . . In truth we are not now considering merely a vocabulary
> or its derivation; we are discussing the *ideas* which suggested and developed
> the terms that symbolise them, and the empirical source of those ideas.
>
> (Welby, 1907, 383)

Welby is arguing that as *all* temporal language derives from spatial language,
our idea of time must derive from our idea of space. More deeply, she is
concerned with the 'empirical source' of these ideas.

We can flesh out this thesis by looking to the Welby–Peirce correspondence.
In a letter dated 16 December 1904, Peirce (repr. in Hardwick, 1977, 47)
comments on a draft of 'Time as Derivative' and poses an objection to it:
even if Welby is right that temporal language depends on spatial language,
this *only* proves time's dependence on space 'in speech'. Welby (repr. in
Hardwick, 1977, 51) replies on 7 January 1905 that our lack of temporal
vocabulary shows we lack 'experience' of time, and 'for the best of reasons:
that time is a product of space + motion – is in fact a kind of space'. Petrilli
(2009, 393) helpfully characterises their exchange, explaining that, for Peirce,
'linguistic usage did not offer proof of the derivative character of time'. But, for
Welby, it did: she believed that 'linguistic expression is indicative of the
functioning of our mental categories and modelling of experience'. The linguistic dependence of time on space shows a conceptual dependence of time on
space and, as our concepts are drawn from experience, this indicates that we
lack experience of time.

Welby's view that our language and concepts of time are drawn from space anticipates some twenty-first-century neuroscience. Buonomano's (2017, 179–94) discussion, 'The Spatialization of Time in Neuroscience', amasses evidence to show 'that the brain itself spatializes time': studies show children require a concept of space before they can understand time; we 'often use spatial terms to talk about time' such that English speakers 'place the past behind us and the future in front'; and 'Spatial metaphors are often used to talk about time, but temporal metaphors are rarely used to describe space.' He even wonders if the brain's spatialisation of time predisposes us towards a block universe theory, in which, as Buonomano (2017, 12) puts it, 'the past and future are as real as locations north and south of you'. Had this research existed in the early twentieth century, I have no doubt Welby would have cited it as support for her position.

Moving on, §IV of 'Time is Derivative' considers the empirical sources of our experience:

> I conceive that the idea of Time has arisen because . . . realising, experience in its aspect as a sequence of change, we need to measure it. Borrowing a space idea for the purpose, we measure it as a line . . . but it is only a metaphorical application of a space-idea, and for that reason has (as we have seen) to be content with an entirely borrowed vocabulary . . . Time . . . is in fact but an inference or a translation found expedient in practice, and has no existence in the sense in which Space has existence. (Welby, 1907, 393–4)

Above, it was implied that our idea of time *lacks an empirical source*; here, we are told that time itself *has no existence* in the sense that space does. This passage lays the foundation for my reading of 'Time as Derivative'. All *realisms* about time, including 'A-theory' and 'B-theory', order events by before and after. Additionally, A-theorists order events by present, past, and future. *Anti-realisms* about time hold that nothing is before or after (and certainly not past, present, or future). As I read Welby, she offers full-blown anti-realism about time.

Unlike our idea of time, she holds that our idea of space *does* have an empirical source: our perception of space and motion, via change. 'Change', Welby (1907, 396) writes, 'seems to be the central or original experience'. At this point, it is helpful to recognise that, for Welby, all changes are motions. She makes this point clearly in an unpublished note titled 'Motion', dated July 1900:

> [A]t present we have but a restricted or working idea [of motion], – that of the so-called physicist. Motion from that point of view is the change of position (e.g. of energy but no matter of what). But I want a word to cover the movement implied in any kind of change; of direction, of bulk, of colour, of shape, &c in space and in time. To me change itself is a fact which belongs

to the order of which Motion is the physicist's example. It is motion in this enlarged sense with which we have to begin.[89]

If you think that all change is a kind of motion, then of course you would hold that, whenever we perceive change, we perceive motion.

§IV continues:

> Time is really the translation of diversity-*in*-position, through change-*of*-position, into succession; and is the effect of a mental condition corresponding to the pre-visual stage of sense-perception. Just as the blind man cannot see at once the scheme of objects, the 'scape' before him, but must touch one object after the other ... so we cannot 'see' the Time-scheme as we can see the Space-scheme together in one act: and thus we erect 'past, present, future' ... and tap our way through life, touching as it were each 'moment', each unit of the Time- space. (Welby, 1907, 395)

A little later, Welby (1907, 398) distinguishes two 'modes' of motion or change in space: 'the successive' and 'the simultaneous'. To illustrate, she writes that you can strike two musical notes 'successively or simultaneously'. I read Welby as claiming that we experience two kinds of change: simultaneous variety or 'diversity-*in*-position', such as a garden holding many kinds of plants; and temporal succession or 'change-*of*-position', such as a sprout growing into a sapling. Simultaneous variety is obviously a kind of change over space: the flowers are red here, and yellow there. Yet as I understand Welby, temporal succession is *also* a kind of change over space: the tree is a sprout here, and a sapling there. Strictly speaking, there is no *temporal* succession – it's just a 'translation' of simultaneous variety in space. But we have a 'mental condition' that prevents us from seeing the sprout and the bush spatially, as existing together. Welby's blind man cannot see the simultaneous variety of a garden, or any 'Space-scheme', as the 'one act' it really is: he can only 'touch' each plant in succession. Similarly, we cannot see the life of a tree, or any 'Time-scheme', as the 'one act' it really is: we can only touch each moment of time in succession. For Welby (1907, 397), our 'mental blindness ... creates the successive'. In effect, our mental blindness creates time.

Given Welby's view that humans 'erect' past, present, and future, she is evidently not an A-theorist. Yet many of her claims are compatible with B-theory, which can be characterised more fully as follows:

> B-theorists think all change can be described in before-after terms. They typically portray spacetime as a spread-out manifold with events occurring at different locations in the manifold. ... Living in a world of change means living in a world with variation in this manifold. ... [An] autumn leaf changed color ... [if] the

---

leaf is green in an earlier location of the manifold and red in a later location. The locations … are specific times in the manifold. (Emery et al., 2020, §5)

On 'typical' B-theories, ours is a block universe: it is an existing whole, a spread-out manifold of events, and there is no privileged present. On my reading of 'Time as Derivative', Welby's universe is a block, but it is *not* B-theorist. This is because, for Welby, our idea of time lacks an empirical source, and time does not exist outside our minds. Everything is really in space, but nothing is really in time. On this reading, there are two key differences between B-theory and Welby's anti-realism.

One concerns the nature of the block manifold. For the B-theorist, the manifold is space-time: a leaf is green at one location in the manifold and red at another – and these locations are *times*. In contrast, Welby's manifold is space, and its locations are *spatial positions*. I find confirmation of this in the way that Welby conceives the past and future as spatial locations. For example, in §V of 'Time as Derivative', Welby (1907, 400) describes the past as 'the world already explored by Man on his great journey through the life-country', and the future as 'that which is yet below a given horizon … the world waiting for him'. She is even more explicit in a letter to Peirce dated 20 November 1904:

I wish instead of the Future we could begin to talk of the Unreached as the Yet distant! We do already talk of the near or distant future; and 'future' itself like *all* the time-words is non-temporal. It is just the *Beyond now*; and the now is essentially the here. (Welby, repr. in Hardwick, 1977, 40)

For Welby, the 'future' is simply a spatial location, beyond her location. The years 1907 and 2107 are not times separated by a temporal distance, but spaces separated by a spatial distance.

The other key difference concerns the temporal relations *before* and *after*. For the B-theorist, events really occur *before* or *after* each other. On my reading, Welby denies this. As she puts it in the passage immediately above, *all* time-words are non-temporal. For Welby, nothing really happens before or after, because time is merely spatial 'diversity-*in*-position'. This is why Welby (1907, 385) characterises before and after as spatial positions: '"before" is before a man in a place, on a spot, in Space, and "after" is what follows or remains behind him'. Her 1909 paper makes this point exceptionally clearly:

We may agree that 'the relations of earlier and later are permanent'. But why? Because they are questions of position. (Welby, 1909, 326)

For Welby, a leaf changes colour from August to September in *exactly* the same way different parts of a single leaf can be smooth and rough: change is diversity across space. For the B-theorist, a world without conscious beings would still be

Figure 8 Illustrating change across space, through patches of ocean

temporal. As Bertrand Russell (1915, 212) once wrote, 'In a world in which there was no experience there would be no past, present, or future, but there might well be earlier and later.' In contrast, given her view that time is only a mind-dependent idea, I argue that for Welby a world without conscious beings would not be temporal. In comments on a draft of 'Time as Derivative', Welby's friend William MacDonald puts her view exactly like this: 'Before there was sentient being, there was matter extended and movable in space ... but not in time, because ... there was no Time until sentient being invented it.'[90] This is not B-theory, but anti-realism.

To better understand this reading of Welby, it will be helpful to illustrate it. Consider Figure 8. Imagine these three squares are patches of ocean: one patch is calm and clear; another is darker; and the last, perhaps close to rocks, is rough and black. This is an example of simultaneous change: variation across space. Now imagine one patch of ocean, gradually darkening from daytime to dusk to midnight. This is an example of successive change: what we usually call change as across time. But, for Welby, this is simply another kind of change across space. It is difficult to represent successive change using still images, but late-nineteenth-century photographers developed ways of doing just that – and, I argue, Welby approved their spatial representations of what we usually call time.

§IV of 'Time as Derivative' hints at how we could see the world, if not for our mental blindness with regards to time:

> But for this disability, we could at will not only dissolve a picture into its successive acts of painting or into its constituent factors (which by means of photography we can now do) but we could even hear a symphony ... as one transcendent Chord. (Welby, 1907, 399)

I'll take these illustrations in reverse order. A group of musical notes can be played successively, say as an arpeggio; or simultaneously, as a chord. Welby is saying that we usually hear a symphony successively, yet, if we could perceive the world as it really is, we would hear it is as a single chord. Welby previously used the example of a chord in her 1897–1900 "Paraphrase of a parallel

---

[90] The summary is held in an envelope postmarked 1906; see VWF, 1970–010/032–04.

Figure 9 'Arab horse at a gallop'. Photograph by Jules Marey. This image is in the public domain, courtesy of Wikipedia Commons (https://en .wikipedia.org/wiki/File:%C3%89tienne-Jules_Marey_-_Arab_ Horse_Gallup_-_Google_Art_Project.jpg)

definition of Time + Space". Meanwhile, the reference to photography we can 'now' do almost certainly refers to Victorian inventions such as 1860s 'chronophotography', which captured motion through successive images, such as Étienne-Jules Marey's horses in Figure 9. Chronophotography arguably spatialises time, by portraying a temporal process (such as painting) as a spatial series. Welby's personal papers include a 1904 *Nature* clipping about Rina Scott's pioneering time-lapse photography of plants. Scott photographed plants growing across days or weeks, and showed their growth on screen across a few seconds. For example, Scott (1903, 780) showed the flowers of *Sparmannia Africana* slowly unfurling. On her clipping, Welby notes, 'Thus time can be telescoped or microscoped. But space, its source ... cannot.'[91] Like Alice in Wonderland, time can be made longer or shorter, but space cannot.

Welby's approval of photography demands a detour into the work of French philosopher Henri Bergson,[92] who famously rejected the spatialisation of time, and critiqued these photographic techniques. For example, in his 1889 *Essai sur les données immédiates de la conscience* (*Time and Free Will*), Bergson (1910, 98) critiques accounts of time that fall 'back upon space ... really giving up time'. Bergson's 1907 *L'Évolution créatrice (Creative Evolution)* argues that chronophotography, and the new art of cinematography, depict time spatially, and hence fail to capture the true nature of time. For example, Bergson (1911, 351) writes, 'Of the gallop of a horse our eye perceives chiefly a characteristic, essential ... form.' In contrast, 'instantaneous photography' 'spreads out' the horse's gallop, portraying

---

[91] The original newspaper clipping lies in VWF, 1970–010/032–07. Welby had a duplicate made, and it is this she annotated; see VWF, 1970–010/032–08.

[92] For a rare discussion of Welby's reception of Bergson generally, see Schmitz (1985, lxix–lxx).

mere 'quantitative variations'. Bergson did not publish on photography before 1907,[93] so Welby was probably unaware of his views when she wrote 'Time as Derivative'; had she known, I imagine she would have rebutted them. For Welby, these kinds of photographs capture the truth: a horse's motion *is* variation across space.

Given their dissenting views on the spatialisation of time, it is prima facie puzzling that §III of 'Time as Derivative' includes excerpts from Bergson's *Time and Free Will* that Welby takes to *support* her position. She places these alongside excerpts from another French text, Jean-Marie Guyau's 1890 *La genèse de l'idée de temps* (*The Genesis of the Idea of Time*). Welby (1907, 392–3) notes that she became 'acquainted' with these texts after writing her paper, but they are important because 'they are in a substantial agreement with its contention'. She quotes Bergson's description of time as a 'bastard concept' (*concept batard*), resulting from the intrusion of an idea of space into consciousness. She also quotes Guyau's description of time as a 'simple effect of consciousness' (*simple effet de la donscience*), and his thesis that language shows our idea of time to be the product of evolution (*La philologie indique donc une evolution de l'idee de temps*). The commonality Welby finds with Guyau's position is obvious – and it suggests Welby endorses the thesis that we evolved our idea of time. But what is the commonality she finds with Bergson? I find Lovejoy's (1912, 527) analysis of Guyau and Bergson helpful here: he writes that they 'reached at least one common conclusion ... our ordinary notions of time are deeply infected with imagery derived from our experiences of space'. Lovejoy explains that they use this conclusion differently: Guyau takes it as a 'clue' regarding the spatial genesis of time perception, whereas Bergson argues that space-infected time is false time, and accordingly finds Guyau's genesis theory 'inadmissible'. Although Welby is ultimately on Guyau's side, she shares Guyau and Bergson's 'common conclusion'. Our notion of time *is* deeply infected by space. And, for Welby, that is exactly as it should be: time is just a kind of space.

An advantage of my reading of Welby is that, I argue, it helps us makes sense of other 1900s texts within her corpus. For example, in a 1903–5 letter to Edmund McClure, Welby (repr. in Cust, 1931, 131–2) writes that the 'origin' of time is 'space-motion': 'The space of succession which we call "time" is of course as much space as the space of the simultaneous.' For Welby, time is a kind of space. I find she makes the same point in a 1903–5 letter to W. R. Sorley, in the context of discussing a draft of 'Time as Derivative'. She states that, on her hypothesis:

---

[93] See Canales (2015, 285, note 6), who also provides discussion of Bergson's views on chronophotography and film.

time is a derivative from space, and may even be called kind of space . . . Time may be described as a special way of dealing with space-ideas, and of applying them to experience. . . . With regard to what you say of the critic's probable objection that we have already assumed time when we assume change or succession . . . when we look at a hill-side covered with successive rows of terraces or houses or trees, etc., we do not mean succession in time but in space, its original home. Again, we may illustrate what is meant by change and succession before time comes in, as what the critic of a picture notices when he compares the different parts of what is still a simultaneous whole. He speaks of the change in size and tint which distant effects – the near hill green, the far one blue; he speaks of the sequence of lines in the picture . . . there is no question whatever of time in this either. (Welby, repr. in Cust, 1931, 134–5)

On Welby's account of time, time is a kind of succession in space. In a response to a worry Sorley raises, that any kind of succession assumes time, Welby replies that succession *can* be purely spatial: take the succession of trees on a hillside, or changes in colour within a painting. What we describe as succession in time is *really* succession 'in space, its original home'. As Welby puts it in a note authored on 27 April 1907, her 70th birthday: '70 years <u>of</u> what? Of life, experience . . . 70 years <u>in</u> what? Space'.[94]

Figure 7 illustrates Welby's description of her block universe, taken from her unpublished 1910 essay 'The Significs of Space and Time'. The essay uses her description to advance her spatial understanding of time:

Let a circle symbolise space and let a row of dots in it represent, as a whole, Time . . . thus space includes time as its subordinate, just as it includes material contents. In Time we are restricted, except ideally and conceptually (a large exception), to a forward movement in a given direction . . .

The thin mental skin separating us from the full recognition that time is included in space . . . is wearing thinner. It can hardly be long now before we realise that what we <u>leave behind</u> or recognise as <u>passed by</u> in the journey of life, in the history of man, is no more lost to us than an object in space to which we may return by reversing our movement or by going round a world.[95]

This passage makes several claims. It reiterates Welby's block universe theory: events in the past are no more lost to us than objects are in another part of space. It also states that space *includes* time, just as it includes its material contents; I argue this fits with my reading of time as a kind of space. Finally, this passage recognises that we are not 'ideally and conceptually' restricted to travelling forwards in time. I suspect this is a reference to stories about time travel, a subject to which we now turn.

---

[94] VWF, 1970–010/032–01.   [95] VWF, 1970–010/032–02.

7.5 The Victorian 'Fourth Dimension'

To better understand what I take to be the main thesis of 'Time as Derivative', that time is a kind of space, I argue we should read it as growing out of Victorian debates around the 'fourth dimension'. Section 3.2 described the fourth dimension as a dimension of space. In a wide variety of ways, some 1880s thinkers came to conceive the fourth dimension as time.[96] For example, in a *Nature* article titled 'Four-Dimensional Space', a mysterious writer 'S' (1885, 481) explicitly considers 'Time as a fourth dimension': 'Since this fourth dimension cannot be introduced into space, as commonly understood, we require a new kind of space for its existence, which we may call time-space.' Wells' *The Time Machine* popularised the notion that time is the fourth dimension, by having his time traveller explain:

> There are really four dimensions, three which we call the three planes of Space, and a fourth, Time ...
>   Scientific people ... know very well that Time is only a kind of Space. (Wells, 1895, 7, 10)

For Wells' (1895, 5) characters, this enables time travel: 'admit that time is a spatial dimension ... it becomes possible to travel about in time'. Arthur (2019, 40) helpfully explains Wells' reasoning: a subject 'moves in three dimensions of space and one of time' but, 'because the time dimension is really a spatial dimension of a different kind, the subject may move forward or back along this dimension at different rates'.

Welby was closely familiar with discourse around the fourth dimension, and with the thesis that it should be identified with time. In addition to *Flatland*, Welby owned at least two other books covering the fourth dimension: Hinton's 1888 *New Era of Thought*, and Alfred Taylor Schofield's 1888 *Another World; or, the Fourth Dimension*.[97] In a letter to Pollock dated 3–4 December 1887, she even states, 'some years ago I passed through what might perhaps be called a Hinton phase'.[98] Interestingly, Wells (cited in Ruddick, 2001, 243) wrote that *Flatland* 'started' him writing *The Time Machine*.

With regard to time as the fourth dimension, Welby's 1891 correspondence with Lodge is of especial interest. In 1891, Lodge gave an address, subsequently published in *Nature*:

> A luminous and helpful idea is that *time* is but a relative mode of regarding things; we progress through phenomena at a certain definite pace, and this

---

[96] On this history, see Bork (1964), Nahin (1993, 89–97), and Throesch (2017, 26–32, 48–53, 133–7).
[97] The Lady Welby Library catalogue, University of London.   [98] VWF, 1970–010/013.

subjective advance we interpret in an objective manner, as if events necessarily happened in this order and at this precise rate. But that may be only one mode of regarding them. The events may be in some sense existent always, both past and future, and it may be we who are arriving at them, not they which are happening. The analogy of a traveller in a railway train is useful. If he could never leave the train or alter its pace, he would probably consider the landscapes as necessarily successive, and be unable to conceive their co-existence . . .

We perceive, therefore, a possible fourth dimensional aspect about time, the inexorableness of whose flow may be a natural part of our present limitations . . . [but] past and future may be actually existing. (Lodge, 1891, 386)

Lodge's 'luminous' idea, that events may be 'existent always', is of course the kind of block universe theory shared by Welby. In a letter to Lodge dated 22 September 1891, Welby recounts annotating his address 'from end to end', and her friends saying, 'why, that is just what you have been trying for years to make us understand!'. In a reply dated 19 November 1891, Lodge restates his view, writing that 'time' is 'like a 4th dimension of space being traversed by us at a perfectly constant pace'. Welby replies on 2 December 1891:

[Y]our own thought of it [time] does all I want, which is to undermine the artificial barriers . . . created by the ordinary notions of 'time' . . . as all our terms for time are borrowed from one-dimensional space only, would it not seem likely that we are in a sort of 'Line-Land' in time answering or comparable somehow, as you suggest, to a fourth dimension in space?[99]

Linelanders perceive one dimension of space, yet there is more to space. We only perceive one dimension of time yet, Welby suggests, there is more to time. Picking up on Lodge's suggestion, Welby speculates that our 'Line-Land' of time is, or is similar to, a fourth spatial dimension. Notably, this is the same letter in which Welby invites Lodge to visit Denton for her Easter 1892 gathering; she writes that they should particularly discuss his 'memorable Address'. I argue this letter bears on the origins of Welby's mature metaphysic in two ways: it contains (what I believe to be) her earliest suggestion that time may be a kind of space; and it is connected with discourse around the fourth dimension. I argue this discourse powers her mature account of time.

Welby even connects her mature account with time travel. In her first letter to Wells, dated 18 November 1897, Welby applauds his 'inimitable' *Time Machine*.[100] They corresponded until 1910, and Wells probably visited her; one of Wells' novels refers to 'Lady Welby's work upon Significs'.[101]

---

[99] VWF, 1970–010/009.   [100] VWF, 1970–010/019–19.
[101] See Schmitz (1985, clxxxiv–clxxxv).

Frustratingly, their extant correspondence does not further discuss time or *The Time Machine*, but I wonder what Wells would have made of her metaphysic. Welby clearly felt an affinity between their views. In the published version of 'Time as Derivative', Welby (1907, 400) concludes §V by stating we must explore new, future 'continents' of Time. But the 1902 draft adds:

> This line of thought of course links itself to the theme of Mr. Wells' vivid romance of the Time Machine. He at least seems to see how elementary as yet our grasp of the possibilities of the 'time-space' are.[102]

Perhaps this conclusion did not make it into the published version because Welby worried that referencing science fiction might make her philosophy appear fanciful. Whatever happened to it, this draft conclusion provides further evidence that Welby's account of time as a kind of space draws from Victorian fourth dimension discourse. An excised passage from *The Time Machine* states:

> To an omniscient observer ... present and past and future would be without meaning. ... He would see ... a Rigid Universe filling space and time. ... If 'past' meant anything, it would mean looking in a certain direction, while 'future' meant looking the opposite way. (Wells, cited in Nahin, 1993, 113)

This passage would fit seamlessly into 'Time as Derivative'. As I read her, Welby agrees with the likes of McTaggart that 'reality is one timeless whole', yet she reaches this conclusion via an alternative route – a fourth dimensional understanding of space. Welby has put a metaphysic to the Wellsian zeitgeist.

8 Motion-Space

Throughout our discussion of Welby's later texts on time, readers may have noticed that she continually connects Motion with space. For example, in her 1897–1900 table of space–time parallels, she refers to 'motion-space'; in a 1903–5 letter to McClure, to 'space-motion'; and in a 1905 letter to Peirce, to 'space + motion'. I have not found any earlier references in Welby's corpus, indicating that she did not make this connection until the late 1890s. This section asks how best to understand it.

Welby's most detailed statements concerning Motion-Space occur in 'Time as Derivative':

> [W]hereas Space is the primary and inevitable 'Room' for change, motion, sequence, succession, measure, number and direction, Time is the product of our experience of Motion and its condition, Space ...
> what else is Space but Room for all else? (Welby, 1907, 383)

---

[102] VWF, 1970–010/032–03.

Space is the 'room' which everything occupies, including change and motion. The implication is that everything which exists, exists in space. As such, space is a precondition for anything to exist. I take this to be what Welby means by her claim that space is the 'condition' of Motion. Some confirmation of this can be found in an untitled essay by Welby, dated 13 July 1907. Having described Space as the 'condition' of Motion, the essay adds that as such Space 'serves for', or is the 'means of' Motion.[103]

However, 'Time is Derivative' goes further than this:

> Space itself is really one with Motion. They cannot be put asunder either sensibly or rationally. *We need a word which shall combine the two conceptions* ... [for] the conception of Motion-Space. (Welby, 1907, 398)

How should we understand this? Section 3.3 argued that Welby's Motion grew out of several vortex theories of matter. Here, I argue that another such theory offers a way to understand Motion-Space. As Doran (1975, 197) notes, one unusual vortex theory conceives matter as motions of *space*.

W. K. Clifford advances this theory in an 1870 talk, 'On the Space-theory of Matter'; all that remains of it is an abstract, reprinted in his 1882 *Mathematical Papers*. The abstract compares parts of space with 'little hills', and writes:

> [T]his property of being curved or distorted is continually being passed on from one portion of space to another after the manner of a wave ...
> this variation of the curvature of space is what really happens in that phenomenon in which we call the motion of matter ...
> in the physical world nothing else takes place but this variation. (Clifford, 1882, 22)

For Clifford, matter is identical with the curvature of space.

We have already seen that Welby was familiar with Clifford's panpsychism, and there is ample evidence that she was also familiar with his space theory of matter. For example, in the 1889–90 letter to McClure describing ideas she has had 'all or nearly all my life' that are now in 'correspondence' with science, Welby (repr. in Cust, 1929, 265–6) includes 'The curvature of space'. In the same letter, she writes, 'it was the Essays of Professor Clifford that first caused me, so to speak, to begin all my thinking from the other end'. Furthermore, Karl Pearson's (1892, 323) *Grammar of Science* discusses Clifford's theory, describing a material body as a 'wrinkle' in space. In her notes on this, Welby describes Clifford's theory without criticising it.[104] I argue this offers a path towards Motion-Space. We know that Welby endorsed Karl Pearson's position that

---

[103] VWF, 1970–010/31–04. This is reprinted in Petrilli (2009, 515–16).
[104] VWF, 1970–010/22–06.

material bodies are modes of motion, akin to 'waves'. For Pearson, they are waves of ether, but it is surely only a short step to Clifford's position that material bodies are waves of space.

Finally, I cannot resist highlighting a passage in Clifford's *Lectures and Essays* – the volumes that Welby read so closely – which eerily prefigures Welby's later writings on space, motion, and time. In the context of describing our perception of motion, such as the motions of a train and its passengers, Clifford writes that our experience is supplemented by 'the laws of kinematic, or of the pure science of motion'. He adds:

> [S]ome of these rules are the foundations of the pure sciences of Space and Motion.
>   Instead of Space and Motion, many people would like to say Space and Time. But ... it seems to me, for reasons which I do not wish to give at present, to be more correct to say that we imagine time by putting together space and motion, than that we imagine motion by putting together space and time. (Clifford, 1879, vol. 1, 262)

Clifford does not explain his meaning, and he may simply be explaining how we develop the science of motion, rather than making any kind of metaphysical statement.[105] But I cannot help but wonder if it inspired Welby nonetheless.

9 Final Thoughts: Motion and God

Pulling this study together, I summarise my reading of Welby's metaphysics as follows. At its heart lies Motion, the dynamic collection of motions comprising the material universe. In Welby's early work, she conceives Motion as energy. Energy is a kind of spirit, so Welby is ultimately an idealist. Motions or waves within Motion give rise to material bodies and minds. Driven by her view that human minds are akin to the rest of the earth, Welby defends a form of panpsychism: 'mind-activity' or 'metakinesis' floods the universe, a kind of 'pre-consciousness-which-is-not-yet-consciousness-but-which-may-develop-into-consciousness'. Yet, I argue, her panpsychism is complicated by her recognition that life and mind are novelties that only appear with certain 'levels' in reality. Welby's struggle to accommodate such novelties run parallel to those of later evolutionary emergentists. Across her career, Welby conceives the universe as a block, extended in space and time. Just as London and Beijing exist, so too do the years 3000 BCE and 3000 CE. From around 1897, Welby develops a new metaphysic of time, on which time

---

[105] I am grateful to Bill Mander, an expert on Clifford, for informal discussion on this point.

is a kind of space. All change, whether occurring simultaneously (such as from one patch of garden to another) or occurring successively (such as a seed growing into a sapling), is variation across space. From around the same period, Welby claims that space is a condition of Motion, that we should even identify the two as Motion-Space. On this view, waves in Motion-Space produce matter and minds. This system is speculative but, as we have seen, it is fuelled by the physics and biology of her period.

By way of concluding this study, I'll say a little on how Welby's metaphysics connect with her philosophy of religion. Scholars have long recognised that Welby was deeply religious.[106] Section 5 saw Welby describe the Christian Holy Spirit as 'the moving and governing force – the Prime Mover'. How does Welby understand the relationship between Motion and God?

The 1902 draft of 'Time as Derivative' contains a passage which does not survive in the published version, stating that Motion points towards God:

> What we see as Motion in the physical world is the most elementary form ... of, that which is even higher than the activity which we call the power of Free Initiative or Efficient will ... Motion which involves the idea of order on the highest conceivable plane is that towards which all forms of energy or activity point, and for which (except in the religious sphere) we have yet no word.[107]

Welby seems to describe a hierarchy of motion or activity: physical motion is lower than conscious activity, and the highest kind of conscious activity which is free will. Yet all these motions or activities are merely 'forms' of something 'even higher', which is presumably why they 'point' to something on the 'highest conceivable plane'. Welby does not tell us exactly what that something is, but the fact it can be described 'in the religious sphere' implies that it is God.

The notion that God is the highest form of motion or activity might seem peculiar, for traditionally God is said to be immutable – unchanging. Speculatively, I suggest Welby may connect God with Motion as follows. In the 1902 draft, the passage above is quickly followed by a suggestion (which does survive in the published version) that 'Motion ... may be taken to symbolise the most inclusive concept possible to us, allying itself to that of "energeia"'. In the

---

[106] On Welby's theism more generally, especially as it relates to her views on language, see Schmitz (1985, xxviii–xxxvii) and Petrilli (2009, 152–67).

[107] VWF, 1970–010/032–03.

paper, Welby doesn't explain what she means by this, but I have found that she discusses energeia in another place: her correspondence with Schiller.

The Greek term *energeia* is perhaps best translated as 'activity'.[108] In October 1900, Schiller published a paper on Aristotle's account of energeia; in advance of that, he gave a draft of the paper to Welby. In the article, Schiller (1900, 458–60) describes 'process' views of the world as those which affirm 'the ultimate reality of Becoming, the unlimited all-pervading Process'. Schiller reads Aristotle as advancing a process view on which energeia is key. On this reading, Aristotle establishes the importance of energeia by pointing out that 'a substance apart from its activity is an abstraction … to *be* is to *be active*'. Aristotle's account of energeia includes *kinesis* – motion. Yet, on Schiller's reading, energeia 'does not essentially necessarily imply motion or change'. For example, God's 'inexhaustible' energeia is 'above and beyond' kinesis: 'for there is not only an activity of motion, but also one void of motion … and pleasure is rather in constancy than in motion'. Schiller (1900, 461) wryly concludes that the 'divine life is one of unceasing and unchanging activity … yet nothing *happens* in it'.

In a letter dated 10 July 1900, Welby sent Schiller comments on his draft of this paper, describing it as 'striking', and adding she 'read it with the keenest interest'. In her comments, it becomes apparent that she is borrowing Schiller's understanding energeia for her own ends:

> To be is to be active. Exactly. Not to exist or to persist, except to be the condition, the cause, the 'Fount' of Motion and Change. … But then what moves? Now this question has two senses:
>
> 1. What piece of matter or what substance is moving?
> 2. What motor or motive moves it?
>
> Have we a word for the answer?
>
> Exactly. Aristotle's Energeia comes near to what I ask for, and does include kinesis. So as Lord Armstrong says, It is Energy not Matter which is moved.[109]

This passage states that the question, 'What moves?' has two senses: what is moving, and what moves it? Both senses of this question have the same one-word answer: energeia. Welby seems to understand energeia as energy, which is why she references Armstrong's thesis that it is energy that moves. In other words, Welby is claiming it is energy that is moving, and energy is also the cause of that movement. This fits with what we already know of Welby's metaphysic of Motion. What is new is the potential this offers for understanding God's place within her system.

---

[108] On the translation, and more recent readings of Aristotle on energeia, see Cohen and Reeve (2021, §12).
[109] VWF, 1970–010/014–05.

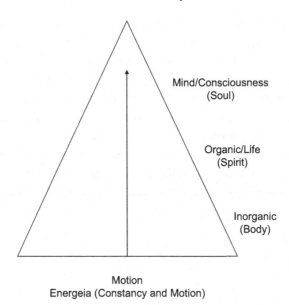

Motion
Energeia (Constancy and Motion)

Figure 10 Levels within Welby's metaphysics, supplemented

She writes that Aristotle's energeia 'does include' kinesis – but, by implication, is not exhausted by it. This suggests that, as on Schiller's interpretation of energeia, she is open to a form of energeia that is 'void of motion'.

And perhaps, borrowing further from Schiller, this is how Welby understands God's relationship with Motion. His 'inexhaustible' energeia comprises the 'Fount' of Motion and change. The Biblical book of *Acts* (17:28) writes of God, 'For in him we live and move and have our being'. Welby paraphrases this in a letter to Norman Pearson dated 20 October 1886: 'We live and move and have our being in the *source* of all generation, evolution, action, and development' (my emphasis).[110] With this in mind, we can modify our representation of Welby's universe: see Figure 10. Welby's universe of Motion is sourced in a divine being that does not change, does not move.

Portraying Welby's God in this way sheds light on other elements of her thought. For example, it helps us better understand why she cares so much that Karl Pearson's account of matter as modes of motion might allow for a mind to be immortal – a philosophy that allows for immortality would appeal hugely to her faith. It helps us better understand her idealism: as God, who is usually conceived as immaterial, is the source of Motion, it follows naturally that

---

[110] VWF, 1970–010/012.

Motion is spirit. It also helps us understand what is fuelling her account of time. Given Welby's stress on motion and the dynamic, readers might be puzzled to find she conceives the universe as a timeless block. Why doesn't she uphold the reality of time and, say, conceive the universe *simpliciter* as changing from moment to moment? Conceiving God as the source of Motion offers an answer. As Welby wrote in *Links and Clues*, if we try to imagine the world from God's perspective, we can briefly penetrate the 'time-veil', 'get *dimly* a glimpse of eternal Fact: the changeless, the solid, the immovable'. God is timeless, and that is why Motion is timeless too. Motion is at the heart of Welby's system, yet her dynamic scheme is moved by an even deeper constant.

References

Abbott, Edwin (1884). *Flatland: A Romance of Many Dimensions*. Seeley: London.

Alexander, Samuel (1920). *Space, Time, and Deity*, 2 volumes. Macmillan: London.

Anonymous (1893). 'New Books', *Mind* 2: 125–35.

Armstrong, Lord (1897a). *Electric Movement in Air and Water: With Theoretical Inferences*. Smith, Elder: London.

(1897b). 'Lord Armstrong on the Supremacy of Motion', *The Times*, 26 August: 6.

(1899). *Electric Movement in Air and Water: With Theoretical Inferences*, 2nd ed., with a supplement. Smith, Elder: London.

Arthur, Richard T. W. (2019). *The Reality of Time Flow: Local Becoming in Modern Physics*. Springer: Cham.

Asprem, Egil (2011). 'Pondering Imponderables: Occultism in the Mirror of Late Classical Physics', *Aries* 11: 129–65.

Bardon, Adrian (2013). *A Brief History of the Philosophy of Time*. Oxford University Press: New York.

Bergonzi, Bernard (1961). *The Early H. G. Wells*. University of Toronto Press: Toronto.

Bergson, Henri (trans. 1910). *Time and Free Will*. George Allen: London.

(trans. 1911). *Creative Evolution*. Macmillan: London.

Blitz, David (1992). *Emergent Evolution*. Kluwer Academic: Netherlands.

Bork, Alfred M. (1964). 'The Fourth Dimension in Nineteenth-Century Physics', *Isis* 55: 326–38.

Bowen, Francis (1877). *Modern Philosophy, from Descartes to Schopenhauer and Hartman*. Scribner, Armstrong: New York.

Bradley, F. H. (1883). *The Principles of Logic*. Kegan Paul, Trench: London.

(1893). *Appearance and Reality: A Metaphysical Essay*. Swan Sonnenschein: London.

Buonomano, Dean (2017). *Your Brain Is a Time Machine: The Neuroscience and Physics of Time*. W. W. Norton: New York.

Canales, Jimena (2015). *The Physicist and the Philosopher: Einstein, Bergson, and the Debate that Changed Our Understanding of Time*. Princeton University Press: Princeton.

Clifford, W. K. (1878). 'On the Nature of Things-in-Themselves', *Mind* 3: 57–67.

(1879). *Lectures and Essays by the Late William Kingdon Clifford*, 2 volumes, edited by Leslie Stephen and Frederick Pollock. Macmillan: London.

(1882). *Mathematical Papers*, edited by Robert Tucker, with an introduction by H. J. Stephen Smith. Macmillan: London.

(1924). 'Victoria Lady Welby: An Ethical Mystic', *The Hibbert Journal* 23: 101–6.

Cohen, S. Marc and C. D. C. Reeve (2021). 'Aristotle's Metaphysics', *The Stanford Encyclopedia of Philosophy*, Edward N. Zalta (ed.). https://plato.stanford.edu/archives/win2021/entries/aristotle-metaphysics/.

Cust, Henry (ed.) (1929). *Echoes of Larger Life: A Selection from the Early Correspondence of Victoria Lady Welby*. Jonathan Cape: London.

(1931). *Other Dimensions: A Selection from the Later Correspondence of Victoria Lady Welby*. Jonathan Cape: London.

Dainton, Barry (2010). *Time and Space*, 2nd ed. Acumen: Durham.

Darwin, Charles (1859). *On the Origin of Species*. John Murray: London.

(1871). *The Descent of Man, and Selection in Relation to Sex*, volume 1. John Murray: London.

Demoor, Marysa (2004). 'Clifford [née Lane], (Sophia) Lucy Jane [pseud. John Inglis] (1846–1929)', *Oxford Dictionary of National Biography*. https://doi.org/10.1093/ref:odnb/57699.

Doran, Barbara Giusti (1975). 'Origins and Consolidation of Field Theory in Nineteenth-Century Britain: From the Mechanical to the Electromagnetic View of Nature', *Historical Studies in the Physical Sciences* 6: 133–260.

Eberty, Felix (1880). *The Stars and the Earth; or, Thoughts Upon Space, Time, and Eternity*, revised by Richard A. Proctor. G. I. Jones: St Louis.

Emery, Nina, Ned Markosian, and Meghan Sullivan (2020). 'Time', *The Stanford Encyclopedia of Philosophy*, Edward N. Zalta (ed.). https://plato.stanford.edu/archives/win2020/entries/time/.

Eschbach, Achim (1983). 'Significs as a Fundamental Science', pp. ix–xxxii, in *What is Meaning?*, edited by Eschbach, with an introductory essay by Gerrit Mannoury and a preface by Achim Eschbach. John Benjamins: Amsterdam.

Forsdyke, Donald R. (2015). '"A Vehicle of Symbols and Nothing More": George Romanes, theory of mind, information, and Samuel Butler', *History of Psychiatry* 26: 270–87.

Guyer, Paul and Rolf-Peter Horstmann (2021). 'Idealism', *The Stanford Encyclopedia of Philosophy*, Edward N. Zalta (ed.). https://plato.stanford.edu/archives/spr2021/entries/idealism/.

Hardwick, Charles S. (ed.) (1977). *Semiotic and Significs: The Correspondence between Charles S. Peirce and Victoria Lady Welby*. Indiana University Press: Bloomington.

Heald, Henrietta (2011). *William Armstrong: Magician of the North*. McNidder and Grace: Alnwick.

Hinton, Charles (1888). *A New Era of Thought*. Swan Sonnenschein & Co: London.

Hoffding, Harald (trans. 1891). *Outlines of Psychology*. Macmillan: New York.

Hunt, Bruce J. (1992). *The Maxwellians*. Cornell University Press: Ithaca.

Hurley, Z. (2022). 'Feminist Pragmatist Salvaging of Victoria Welby's Theory of "Ident"', pp. 55–66, in *Women in Pragmatism: Past, Present and Future*, edited by Núria Sara Miras Boronat and Michela Bella. Springer: Cham.

Ingthorsson, R. D. (2016). *McTaggart's Paradox*. Routledge: New York.

James, William (1882). 'On Some Hegelisms', *Mind* 7: 186–208.

(1884). 'The Dilemma of Determinism', *The Unitarian Review and Religious Magazine* 22: 193–224.

Lloyd Morgan, C. (1890). *Animal Life and Intelligence*. Edward Arnold: London.

(1891). 'Force and Determinism', *Nature* 44: 319.

(1894). *An Introduction to Comparative Psychology*. Walter Scott: London.

(1903). *An Introduction to Comparative Psychology*, 2nd ed. Walter Scott: London.

(1927). *Emergent Evolution*. Williams and Norgate: London.

Lodge, Oliver (1883a). 'The Ether and its Functions I', *Nature*, 25 January: 304–6.

(1883b). 'The Ether and its Functions I', *Nature*, 1 February: 328–30.

(1891). 'Opening Address by Prof. Oliver J. Lodge', *Nature*, 44: 382–7.

Lovejoy, Arthur O. (1912). 'The Problem of Time in Recent French Philosophy III', *The Philosophical Review* 21: 527–45.

Luisi, Maria (2013). 'Space and Time: Continuity in the Correspondence between Charles Peirce and Victoria Welby', *Semiotica* 196: 197–214.

Mander, W. J. (2020). *The Unknowable: A Study in Nineteenth-Century British Metaphysics*. Oxford University Press: Oxford.

McTaggart, J. M. E. (1894). 'Time and the Hegelian Dialectic', *Mind* 3: 190–207.

Metzer, Scott (2020). 'Understanding the Welby-Russell Correspondence', *Dialogue* 59: 579–88.

Misak, Cheryl (2016). *Cambridge Pragmatism: From Peirce and James to Ramsey and Wittgenstein*. Oxford University Press: Oxford.

Myers, William Andrew (1995). 'Victoria, Lady Welby (1837–1912)', pp. 1–24, in *A History of Women Philosophers*, volume 4, edited by Mary Ellen Waithe. Springer: Dordrecht.

Nahin, Paul J. (1993). *Time Machines: Time Travel in Physics, Metaphysics, and Science Fiction*. American Institute of Physics: New York.

(2017). *Time Machine Tales: The Science Fiction Adventures and Philosophical Puzzles of Time Travel*. Springer: Cham.

Nuessel, Frank, Vincent Colapietro, and Susan Petrilli (2013). 'On and Beyond Significs: Centennial Issue for Victoria Lady Welby (1837–1912)', *Semiotica* 196: 1-11.

Owen, W. B. and James G. O'Hara (2004). 'Stoney, George Johnstone (1826–1911), Physicist and University Administrator', *Oxford Dictionary of National Biography*. https://doi.org/10.1093/ref:odnb/36321.

Pearson, James (forthcoming). 'What Welby Wanted', in *Women in the History of Analytic Philosophy*, edited by Jeanne Peijnenburg and Sander Verhaegh. Springer.

Pearson, Karl (1888). *The Ethic of Freethought: A Selection of Essays and Lectures*. T. Fisher Unwin: London.

(1892). *The Grammar of Science*. Walter Scott: London.

(1900). *The Grammar of Science*, 2nd ed. A. & C. Black: London.

Pearson, Norman (1886). 'Before Birth', *The Nineteenth Century* 20: 340–63.

Peijnenburg, Jeanne and Sander Verhaegh (forthcoming). 'Introduction: Women in the History of Analytic Philosophy', in *Women in the History of Analytic Philosophy*. Springer.

Petrilli, Susan (2009). *Signifying and Understanding: Reading the Works of Victoria Welby and the Signific Movement*. De Gruyter Mouton: Berlin.

Pollock, Frederick (1879). 'Introduction', pp. 1–72, in *Lectures and Essays by the Late William Kingdon Clifford*, 2 volumes, edited by Leslie Stephen and Frederick Pollock. Macmillan: London.

Romanes, George J. (1885). 'Mind and Motion', *The Contemporary Review* 48: 74–94.

(1895). *Mind and Motion and Monism*, edited by C. Lloyd Morgan. Longmans, Green: New York.

Ruddick, Nicholas (2001). *The Time Machine: An Invention*. Broadview Press: Peterborough.

Russell, Bertrand (1915). 'On the Experience of Time', *The Monist* 25: 212-233.

S (1885). 'Four-Dimensional Space', *Nature*, 26 March: 481.

Schiller, F. C. S. (1900). 'On the Conception of ΈΝΕ´ΡΓΕΙΑ ΆΚΙΝΗΣΙ´ΑΣ', *Mind* 9: 457–68.

(1901). *Mind! A Unique Review of Ancient and Modern Philosophy*. Williams and Norgate: London.

Schmitz, H. Walter (1985). 'Victoria Lady Welby's Significs', pp. ix–clxxxix, in *Significs and Language*, edited by H. Walter Schmitz. John Benjamins: Amsterdam.

(2013). 'Taking Stock of the Published Correspondence of Victoria, Lady Welby', *Kodikas/Code, Ars Semeiotica* 36: 203–26.

Schofield, Alfred Taylor (1888). *Another World; or, the Fourth Dimension*. Swan Sonnenschein & Co: London.

Scott, Rina (1903). 'On the Movements of the Flowers of Sparmannia Africana, and their Demonstration by Means of the Kinematograph', *Annals of Botany* 17: 761–78.

Smith, Roger (2004). 'Romanes, George John [pseuds. Physicus, Metaphysicus] (1848–1894)', *Oxford Dictionary of National Biography*. https://doi.org/10.1093/ref:odnb/24038.

Spencer, Herbert (1862). *First Principles*. Williams and Norgate: London.

Stephen, Leslie (1893). *An Agnostic's Apology, and Other Essays*. G. P. Putnam's Sons: New York.

Stewart, Balfour and Peter Guthrie Taite (1975). *The Unseen Universe, or Physical Speculations on a Future State*, 2nd ed. Macmillan and Co.: London.

Stone, Alison (forthcoming). *Women Philosophers in Nineteenth-Century Britain*. Oxford University Press.

Stoney, G. Johnstone (1885). 'How Thought Presents Itself in Nature', *Notices of the Proceedings at the Meetings of the Members of the Royal Institution of Great Britain* 11: 178–96.

(1890). 'On Texture in Media, and on the Non-existence of Density in the Elemental Æther', *The London, Edinburgh, and Dublin Philosophical Magazine and Journal of Science* 29: 467–78.

(1903). 'On the Dependence of What Apparently Takes Place in Nature Upon What Actually Occurs in the Universe of Real Existences', *Proceedings of the American Philosophical Society* 42: 105–42.

Sully, James (1892). *The Human Mind: A Text-Book of Psychology*. Longmans, Green: London.

Thomas, Emily (2019). 'The Roots of C. D. Broad's Growing Block Theory of Time', *Mind* 128: 527–49.

(2022). 'Samuel Alexander', *The Stanford Encyclopedia of Philosophy*, Edward N. Zalta (ed.). https://plato.stanford.edu/archives/fall2022/entries/alexander/.

(forthcoming a). 'Mary Calkins, Victoria Welby, and the Spatialisation of Time', *British Journal for the History of Philosophy*.

(forthcoming b). 'Metaphysical Idealists in Britain: Constance Naden, Victoria Welby, and Arabella Buckley', in *Oxford Handbook of*

American and British Women Philosophers in the Nineteenth Century, edited by Alison Stone and Lydia Moland. Oxford University Press.

Thomson, William (1867). 'On Vortex Atoms', *The London, Edinburgh, and Dublin Philosophical Magazine and Journal of Science* 34: 15–24.

(1884). 'Steps Towards a Kinetic Theory of Matter', *Science* 4: 204–6.

Throesch, Elizabeth (2017). *Before Einstein: The Fourth Dimension in Fin-de-Siècle Literature and Culture.* Anthem Press: London.

Wallace, Alfred Russell (1895). *Natural Selection and Tropical Nature: Essays on Descriptive and Theoretical Biology.* Macmillan: London.

Ward, James (1886). 'Psychology', pp. 37–85, in *Encyclopædia Britannica*, 9th ed., volume 20. Charles Scribner's Sons: New York.

Watkins, Eric and Marius Stan (2014). 'Kant's Philosophy of Science', *The Stanford Encyclopedia of Philosophy*, Edward N. Zalta (ed.). https://plato .stanford.edu/archives/fall2014/entries/kant-science/.

Welby, Victoria (1881). *Links and Clues.* Macmillan: London.

(1883). *Links and Clues*, 2nd ed. Macmillan: London.

(1891). 'Breath and the Name of the Soul', *The Open Court* 5: 2893–5.

(1907). 'Time as Derivative', *Mind* 16: 383–400.

(1909). 'Mr. McTaggart on the "Unreality of Time"', *Mind* 18: 326–8.

(1983 [1903]). *What is Meaning?* With an introductory essay by Gerrit Mannoury and a preface by Achim Eschbach. John Benjamins: Amsterdam.

Wells, H. G. (1895). *The Time Machine: An Invention.* Henry Holt: New York.

Woiak, Joanne (2004). 'Pearson, Karl [Formerly Carl] (1857–1936), Statistician and Eugenicist', *Oxford Dictionary of National Biography.* https://doi.org/10 .1093/ref:odnb/35442.

Acknowledgements

This study would not exist save for the preservation efforts of the Victoria Welby Fonds; I owe special thanks to their archivist Jennifer Grant, who helped me access Welby's papers during and after the pandemic. I am also grateful to the AHRC, for funding my trip to Welby's archives; to the Leverhulme Trust, for funding my time on this study; and to two anonymous referees for this journal, one of whom asked especially perspicuous questions about how the different parts of Welby's thought fit together.

Cambridge Elements ≡

Women in the History of Philosophy

Jacqueline Broad
Monash University

Jacqueline Broad is Associate Professor of Philosophy at Monash University, Australia. Her area of expertise is early modern philosophy, with a special focus on seventeenth and eighteenth-century women philosophers. She is the author of *Women Philosophers of the Seventeenth Century* (Cambridge University Press, 2002), *A History of Women's Political Thought in Europe, 1400–1700* (with Karen Green; Cambridge University Press, 2009), and *The Philosophy of Mary Astell: An Early Modern Theory of Virtue* (Oxford University Press, 2015).

Advisory Board

About the Series
In this Cambridge Elements series, distinguished authors provide concise and structured introductions to a comprehensive range of prominent and lesser-known figures in the history of women's philosophical endeavour, from ancient times to the present day.

Cambridge Elements ≡

Women in the History of Philosophy

Elements in the Series

A full series listing is available at: www.cambridge.org/EWHP

Printed in the United States
by Baker & Taylor Publisher Services